A HOSPITAL ODYSSEY

Gwyneth Lewis was Wales's National Poet from 2005 to 2006, the first writer to be given the Welsh laureateship. Her first six books of poetry in Welsh and English were followed by *Chaotic Angels* (Bloodaxe Books, 2005), which brings together the poems from her three English collections, *Parables & Faxes*, *Zero Gravity* and *Keeping Mum*.

Her first collection in English, *Parables & Faxes* (Bloodaxe Books, 1995), won the Aldeburgh Poetry Festival Prize and was shortlisted for the Forward Prize for Best First Collection. Her second, *Zero Gravity* (Bloodaxe Books, 1998), was shortlisted for the Forward Prize for Poetry. The BBC made a documentary of *Zero Gravity*, inspired by her astronaut cousin's voyage to repair the Hubble Space Telescope. Both *Zero Gravity* and *Keeping Mum* (Bloodaxe Books, 2003) were Poetry Book Society Recommendations. *Y Llofrudd Iaith* (Barddas, 1999) won the Welsh Arts Council Book of the Year Prize and *Keeping Mum* was shortlisted for the same prize.

Her latest poetry book, *A Hospital Odyssey* (Bloodaxe Books, 2010), will be followed by a further new collection, *The Sparrow Tree*, in 2011.

Gwyneth Lewis composed the words on the front of Cardiff's Wales Millennium Centre. Her first non-fiction book *Sunbathing in the Rain: A Cheerful Book on Depression* (Harper Perennial, 2002), was shortlisted for the Mind Book of the Year. Her adaptation of the play for BBC Radio 4 won a Mental Health in the Media award. Her second book of non-fiction, *Two in a Boat* (Fourth Estate, 2005) recounts a voyage made with her husband on a small boat from Cardiff to North Africa.

She is a librettist and has written two chamber operas for children, *Redflight/Barcud*, with music by Richard Chew, and *Dolffin*, with music by Julian Phillips. She has also written an oratorio, *The Most Beautiful Man from the Sea*, to music by Orlando Gough and Richard Chew. All were commissioned and performed by Welsh National Opera with amateur singers.

Gwyneth Lewis lives in Cardiff, but has recently spent two years in the US.

GWYNETH LEWIS

A Hospital Odyssey

BLOODAXE BOOKS

Copyright © Gwyneth Lewis 2010

ISBN: 978 1 85224 877 2

First published 2010 by
Bloodaxe Books Ltd,
Highgreen,
Tarset,
Northumberland NE48 1RP.

www.bloodaxebooks.com
For further information about Bloodaxe titles
please visit our website or write to
the above address for a catalogue.

Supported by
**ARTS COUNCIL
ENGLAND**

Cover design: Neil Astley & Pamela Robertson-Pearce.

Printed in Great Britain by
Bell & Bain Limited, Glasgow, Scotland.

To Leighton

My love is faren in a land;
Alas why is he so?
And I am so sore bound
I may not come him to.
He hath my heart in hold
Wherever he ride or go,
With true love a thousand fold.

     Adapted from Anon, 15th century

Dear God
Please bring my husband back home
     EBM

(Prayer book, St Bartholomew's Hospital chapel, London)

BOOK 1

I went to the sea to get oranges,
But that is something the sea does not have.
I returned soaking wet,
Battered this way and that by the waves,
O, my sweet love.

(SPANISH SONG)

'I'll kill you if you die on me now,'
hissed Maris. Her husband Hardy, barely alive,
winced. His trolley's prow
parted Emergency's human waves,
passed luckier patients in curtained caves

and came to rest in a corridor.
She looked, concerned, at his grey-tinged skin.
Shining with fever, his eyes were stars
speeding away from her. A vein
pulsed in his throat. She tried again

to reach him but he'd set sail
without her on an internal sea
and, for all she clutched at the flimsy rail
of his cot, he'd already drifted away,
caught by the current, left her on a quay

alone. She fired emergency flares
of love but it was far too late
to call him back. He was deaf to her,
so she watched him, utterly desolate
as the man she'd married sank from sight

over pain's horizon. He was her compass
in fog, her favourite mountain road,
her eternity ring of precious
stones worth everything, the load
she'd willingly carry. Hardy groaned.

'I'm off to the Pharmacy,' she said,
stroking his cheek. He closed his eyes,
too busy with dying to raise his head.
She found herself saying a silent goodbye
to her husband. She was terrified

he'd be changed for ever, against her will,
by illness. Suddenly she turned a corner
into the concourse, then stood stock still
in wonder. Now I want you to hear
a sound-track: a sci-fi fanfare,

the kind when a novice traveller
sees her first spaceship, takes in with awe
its unimagined scale and grandeur,
the hum of its engines, the sheer power
of sophisticated alien culture.

Maris stood and all around her
people thronged. She was enthralled
by the infinite corridors that converged
like a print by Escher. Market stalls
traded toys and small furry animals

which visitors carried to the unwell.
Long escalators ran in spurs,
moving the healthy as if they were cells
in a greater body, seeking a cure
for themselves or others. It was a fair:

balloons drifted up from the foyer.
Hawkers were pushing dubious pills.
Maris watched a group of tumblers
Performing: 'The Body'. Flexing impressive muscles,
they made her forget her husband's ills

for a moment. Above it all
hung a magnificent chandelier
throwing spangles like the glitter ball
in a disco. Strung on the finest gossamer,
the ever-replenished ornament of tears

was the hospital's primary source of light.
The diamantés fell like dew
on those who gazed up at the dazzling sight.
Distresses formed themselves in new
constellations of glittering sorrow

before they ripened like fruit and fell.
Maris noticed box-lit X-rays
under a sign: *Diagnosis Wall.*
Doctors peered at MRI
scans, each one looking intently

at portraits of internal cavities.
They issued their verdicts. Maris heard
them whispering the simple litany:
'Normal. Not normal.' Then, unperturbed,
they'd stamp a Latin medical word

on a file for consultants. Phials of blood
were being analysed next door.
A robot shook them, thick as mud,
then sampled each glass, a sommelier
guessing a vintage. Maris's eye

was caught by one bottle, which bore the name
of her husband: Hardy. It was ruby red,
an impossible scarlet that caused her alarm
the moment she saw it. Sick with dread,
she watched the gourmet as it tasted,

swilled the wine round its specialist mouth
then spat out the taste of her husband's health.
It hummed and ha'd, its innards whirred
and said it detected 'a soupçon of anaemia'
then worse. It printed the verdict: CANCER.

Maris was stunned. This was a story
that happened to others, not to Hardy and her.
Then she was pierced through with pity
for him, brave man, who'd hidden his terror
of this, the most feared saboteur

of all. Stop reading. If your partner's near
I want you to put this poem down,
surprise them at the morning paper.
Nuzzle their neck. When they ask, 'What's wrong?'
say, 'Nothing,' but hold them close, while you can.

Soon Maris was crying huge snotty sobs,
responding with shock and disbelief
to the verdict, how she'd soon be robbed
of her husband by a cellular thief,
a fifth columnist. Then came grief

and Maris howled, leant into an alcove
and let heartache have its way
with her. Yes, loss is the shadow of love
but it's a scandal that bodies must die,
don't you think? 'My dear, it's not done to cry

like this in public,' a pert voice said.
'Come to my office. We hold a licence
for weeping there. Lucky I spotted
you. There's a particular brilliance
to your sobbing.' The woman was a no-nonsense

bureaucrat. Maris blew her nose
on a proffered tissue. 'Quite a threnody
you produced.' 'It wasn't a show.'
'I think you may be a natural weepie.
A Wednesday's child? There's pots of money

to be made from blubbing, if it's not real.'
Professional weepers sipped sweetened tea
and bawled. 'Not everybody wants to feel
their lives and we find insincerity
does just as well. You have ability,

and could supply a valued service
if you stayed with us. We work in shifts,
on commission. Men are generous.
Some women, we find, give us short shrift
for pretending, like them. They're only miffed

because we've made it professional.
I don't mind some clients on the side
if you're discreet. On the whole,
it's better than cleaning.' 'I think you're sad.
The people who pay you must be mad.

I need the Pharmacy.' But the woman wailed
which raised a chorus of put-on woe,
an ululation which so assailed
Maris's ears she just had to go.
Lost, she wandered to and fro

looking for signs. She asked the way
from a porter who mumbled lazily and waved
in a certain direction and then sashayed
away with his wheelchair. Maris was still naïve
in the ways of this hospital so, when a nave

opened in front of her, she wasn't surprised
but thought, 'I'll sit in this pew for a while
to compose myself.' A musky rose
adorned the altar, its scent narcotic. 'I'll…
just close my eyes.' Her dreams were febrile,

a million tendrils had crossed the floor
and were probing, curious to know
how she tasted. Subtle suckers entered her pores,
were thriving, somehow, on her sorrow.
Branches, engorged now, thick as her torso,

were tying her down. She started awake
to find that taproots had tied her feet
and hands, were fingering her neck.
She struggled against this neural net
but its threads were stout and she pulled the knot

ever tighter, digging in thorns.
This was the hospital's Tree of Pain.
Every cerebral cortex that's born
is part of this sapling. One side is green,
the other burns with the endless flame

of being alive. She was alight
now, could feel the distress of others,
the bush was a thicket and threw a twilight
of inflammation. Its fruit was terror
and horror, the sweetest of blood-red haws.

If you're caught in its web it makes you raw,
broken on prickles. A wave of sympathy
she couldn't block knocked Maris to the floor.
She panicked and thought, 'I've got to get free
or so much feeling is sure to kill me.'

'No it won't.' Two greyhound eyes
stared at her solemnly. 'Let yourself be caught,
it will never harm you.' It seemed wise
to obey. 'Blimey, a talking dog,' she thought.
He countered, 'You're not the crying sort,

I'd say.' Surprise relaxed her and the mesh
fell off her limply. 'Don't try to be separate.
Pain's not the same as unhappiness.
It's not by trying to feel less
you'll escape'. Cords fell from her throat.

Just then the building shifted and sent
everyone flying. 'All aboard
that's sailing!' said the dog and smelt
the air with excitement, quite self-assured.
'The better view, I think, is to starboard,'

the greyhound opined. Now Maris was shrill:
'Who are you and what on earth do you mean?'
The floor vibrated, and Maris could feel
it tilting slightly. 'I am your breathing,
Maris, when something unforeseen

makes you aware of me. Let's go on deck,'
said the dog. 'I like to watch departures.
If I stay below, I always feel sick.
Shouldn't you have gone ashore?'
he asked, with one perfect, white-socked paw

held in the air. Propellers churned.
Her new friend started to wag his tail
and they felt the hospital begin to turn
like an ocean liner setting sail,
the hooter sounding, tooting farewell.

Off-balance, Maris couldn't understand
what was happening. The corridor
lurched, but patiently the hound
Trotted ahead, then waited for her.
They burst together through the fire door

into crowds around the companionway.
The ship, it seemed, had started to pull
away slowly. Friends waved from the jetty,
families cried. Maris turned pale
and screamed 'Get me off this floating hotel!

Where are we going? And where's my man?'
The dog replied, 'He's in another country.'
'Rubbish!' she screamed, 'I demand
to see him now. Stuff you and stuff that scary tree,
stuff this illusion of going to sea,

I want him now.' 'I hope you bought
counterfeit papers. Illness is exile,
Hardy's abroad. You have a passport
but no visa to join him – that is, until
you've cancer yourself. And who can tell

if you'll ever find him?' 'But he's in triage,'
insisted Maris, choking, 'and he's all alone.'
'I doubt it. You're on two voyages,
if you're lucky your parallel lines
will cross. Now you're both on your own,

far from each other.' Maris watched as boats –
no, surely not – they were patients in beds –
slipped their mooring ropes and floated
out to the bay. Above their heads
were helicopters, but patients made

their way in kayaks, some in coracles,
each vessel according to what was wrong
with the owners' bodies, and so their souls
made passage. The sea's so strong,
our craft so frail. Some sang songs

to keep up morale. Some, far offshore
were in heavy weather. Others showed grim
determination, plying their oars.
Maris had to get back to him,
the husband who was her home.

She'd find him, she was so sure.
He was gone. And not a single clue
as to where. Except a Knight Templar
guarding his place, sword in full view.
'Where's Hardy?' she screamed. 'Who the hell are you?'

BOOK 2

The handing over to a stranger the care of a life
precious beyond all computation may be one of
the greatest earthly trials.

WILLIAM OSLER

Many symptoms bear witness to the fact that
medicine, too, is sick.

THORWALD DETHLEFSEN

He sat there, rigid in a straight-backed chair
staring before him. His breast-plate
glinted as he replied: 'I am the Carer
for this bed. What I do is wait
with the patient. You need a knight

for the task, no one else could endure
the endless minutes. This is my quest:
I never ask what the hours are for
but suffer them gladly, like a test
of character which I don't resist –

this boredom's my particular crusade.
Patience, the purest part of love,
is a whetstone, I find, that keeps the mind's blade
sharp in its sheath. I'll never move.
This heavy armour will be my grave,'

he sighed. Like me, this Templar's
a prisoner inside this poem.
Neither of us will get out of here
alive unless I can re-order time
to a second body of words and rhymes.

Right now, I really can't be sure
if I can do it. Grant me first aid –
this epic's an illness that has no cure
but writing it, and I'm afraid
of how it will alter me, what price I'll pay

for my obsession. I'll have to do
what the poem bids me. Charm's
not enough in art, nor is making it new,
so I'll roll up my sleeve and offer my arm
to the muse's needle, a pulsing vein

in exchange for wisdom. 'Where
is my husband?' demanded Maris.
'You mean the man who was just here?'
A honey-bee landed on his shiny cuisse
but he felt nothing. 'He was Number Six

this morning.' 'How can you see
through *that*?' asked Maris. She stared
hard at his helmet. Suddenly
she reached out, flipped up his visor
like a letterbox. He blinked at her.

'If you cared for your patients, then you'd know
where each and every one had gone.'
The Knight returned her look with sorrow.
'Before A&E, I was fully human
but I've learned to live inside this tin can

to stop me feeling. This hospital
consists of guilds. Each treats a part
so nobody sees the person in full,
just specialist sections. The Heart's
a fetish. Cardiacs keep well apart

from Spleens and Kidneys. Oh! My *dear*!'
he exclaimed with delight as Maris tugged
off his helmet. 'Now I can hear
what you're saying! I thought there was fog
on the ward, but it was the fug

in my casque!' Maris reached for his hand,
removed his gauntlet. 'I can't wait
here for my husband. I've got to find
him. Help me. If I were a knight
and armed like you, I'd be willing to fight

for my patients. How can you breathe
inside such armour? How can you move?
He hung his head. 'Once, I was lithe
and limber, but I lost my nerve...'
'Look at me. You're not alive,

you act like a statue. That's not caring,
playing 'Knight of ye Waiting Room,'
not even bothering to stir,
that's not what I call a chivalric doom,
to sit on your armoured arse. No! Time

is nothing, it reports to love.
Help me. I may be completely lost
in this hospital, but I won't leave.
I promise you. Whatever the cost
I'll find him.' Maris knelt and kissed

the Templar's bony hand. A flush
of warmth spread, like an arctic dawn
over his alabaster flesh
and up into his chain-mailed arm
which he raised and flexed, as if in a dream.

'This is what loving forever means:
I love him as he was, he is, will be.
I loved my Hardy before I knew him,
when he was a bare-bottomed baby,
before he thought of loving me.

As a boy when, for Anatomy
exams he became a living model
for students to draw on at the Infirmary.
Or crawling inside his dog Pete's kennel
for animal comfort. When he was a fool

with money before we married. We are one body.
If he's got cancer, then so have I.
At night we dive, dance weightlessly
in clouds of bedclothes. Oh, so calmly
he changes my breathing, drowns me, saves me

time and again.' 'That's indiscreet.'
'Sorry, but I couldn't bear
to lose him. I won't drink or eat
until I've found him again, I swear.
We were meant to be together.'

She bent, untied the straps of the greaves
over his shinbones, then the sabaton,
the gorget, the tasset – like a squire
disarming his master – the couter, the pauldron,
the cuirass, then down to his habergeon

and, lifting his chain mail, she revealed
instead of an insect, a defenceless man.
He looked at himself in his polished shield:
'I know that person. I think I am...
a doctor!' He staggered, clutched at her arm

then straightened. 'My name is Ludlow.
How long was I stuck in that terrible chair?'
He rubbed his limbs to restore the flow
of blood to his muscles. 'I remember
now what I do. I'm a specialist tracker.

My job is to hunt the wild beasts of disease
in every department. But I was laid low
by a sleeping sickness. My lady, please,
how may I serve you?' He bowed
in knightly fashion. 'Just plain Maris will do.

21

There is one thing. Did you see where they sent
my husband? Big man, grumpy but very strong.'
'If I had a pound for each one that went
down that corridor... They're whisked along
quickly, they never tell me where they've gone.

But I'll tell you a secret. I was intrigued, so once
I followed, before I was quite as comatose
as when you found me. Security pounced
on me, but by then I'd been so close
I'd seen what happened. They make you choose.'

'What do you mean?' 'There are three doors
in a hallway. Three ways in
and only one exit. I didn't explore
but I'm sure that they're three ways of being.
'Right,' said Maris, 'that's where I'm going.'

'I'm coming too, you could use a guard,
something's not right in this hospital.
I slept for too long.' She hugged him hard.
He blushed. 'You'll have to choose well
or you'll be a widow if we fail.

Believe me, Maris, your husband's life
depends in large part on what you do.'
'But he's the patient, I'm only his wife...'
'You're fighting for him, a formidable foe,
if I may say so. The sooner we go

the better.' So they made their way
out through the crowds in the entrance hall
where, disregarded, under an archway,
three doors were set in the concourse wall,
three portals that looked identical –

22

but over each lintel a different sign:
Death. Peace. Love. Maris pondered,
'Love? New Age-y. Too anodyne
to save him. *Death?* Too hard,
we want its opposite.' So she moved toward

the door marked *Peace*, took a deep breath.
'Steady, girl,' said a familiar voice.
'Are you sure you shouldn't go for *Death?*'
It was the greyhound, standing close.
'I've come to help you with your choice.'

She smiled, despite herself. Fear
had made her suddenly aware
of breathing. Now she could admire
the sleek black coat, with one white star
on his flank. 'No dogs allowed here,'

she teased him. 'What's your name?'
'Wilson. Mystery Man of the Moors,
he of the body suit and sprinting fame
in *Wizard*. You're Rose and I'm the Doctor!
Anyway, you get the idea.

Let's find your husband.' 'Come here,' said Maris
reaching down to scratch his throat.
'For now, I've chosen this door marked *Peace*.'
She turned the handle and, with his snout,
Wilson pushed. It closed and shut the foyer out.

*

'Sh!' said someone. A row of eyes –
patients tucked up in a general ward,
not daring to move. A reptilian cry,
heads under bedclothes. Fast wings whirred,
brisk round their faces. A colourful bird

landed beside them. It was a woodpecker
nurse. She regarded Maris with a beady eye.
'Who is the patient? Is it her?
I'm Matron. You can leave everything to me.
You're lucky, we have one bed empty.'

And, with undulating flight,
she led the way. 'Now, get undressed,
chop, chop!' she ordered. 'But I'm all right,'
protested Maris. 'Hop in now, or I'll get cross,'
the nurse insisted. 'I'm the boss

and I'm used to patients who obey
instructions.' She opened a file
and started tapping noisily away,
filling in details. 'A female,'
mused Ludlow. 'See, under her tail

are crimson knickers. She's a pied
dendrocopus, a Great
Spotted Woodpecker. 'Open wide,'
the nurse demanded. 'What is your weight?
How are your bowels? Bloods? Heart rate?'

'Hold on!' cried Maris, 'it's my husband who's ill,
not me.' 'N-n-n-nonsense,' Matron stuttered.
'He's poorly, you're married, you have a virtual
disease and, therefore, you have to be cured
of your neuroses. The treatment is hard

but utterly worth it.' 'I must confess,
my body's partnered to his, I do feel sick
if he's laid up.' Obediently, Maris undressed,
pulled on a hospital gown – you know, that classic
backless blue the opposite of chic –

and climbed into bed. 'What are you doing?'
hissed Wilson. 'You're wasting precious time.'
'*She* says I'm ill and I'll do anything
the medics tell me. I'm not to blame,
I have anti-cancer. Ring that buzzer, I'm

feeling queasy.' A little holiday
was all she was after. 'I'm suffering too,'
she thought. 'I'll let my body have its say,
indulge it a little. This feels like 'flu.
Better be careful. It wouldn't do

for me to go down.' 'Cut out the chat!
commanded *dendropocus*. In their cocoons
her patients complied. With a rat-tat-tat
Matron announced: 'Listen up! The Pain
Dispenser's coming!' 'I'll have a migraine,'

someone cried out. 'We have a loyalty card
for regular clients! Rashes going cheap
today! Neuralgia, toothache, nothing too hard
to bear! No, I'm all out of sleeping
sickness. Something minor to stop

anyone nagging? Hypochondriacs!'
she cackled. 'Have a doctor's note
with that. Who ordered this heart attack
for spite? Here's a husky strep throat.'
Then Maris remembered: the pain she sought

belonged to Hardy. 'Here's tinnitus!'
But Maris refused, she'd remembered her quest.
Suffering chosen is very like bliss.
'Here! Matron! I'll take my husband's illness.'
'Pain's not transferable.' She flew to her office

in a huff. 'Matron's Head of Paper.
I've very important forms to fill:
histories, waivers, and disclaimers,
patient pathways and protocols
and...' her speech sped up into a trill

'...they always want it in triplicate.
I'm nothing if not professional.'
Maris grabbed her file, opened her chart.
The paper was punctured by woodpecker braille,
all nonsense. Maris, seeing this, turned pale.

By now the bird was hysterical.
Ludlow came back: 'I've had a wander
and some of these people are really unwell.'
Maris looked round. The man next to her
began to vomit. Nobody stirred

to help him, so Maris attempted to call
the woodpecker nurse. 'Matron! Excuse me!
This man needs help. I think he's soiled
himself.' The nurse looked then flew away
saying, 'N-n-no time! I'm f-f-far too busy!

A patient tried to get up but fell.
Another called out hoarsely for water
and the ward was filled with a shitty smell.
The nurse continued to type, unaware.
'For shame,' shouted Maris, 'you're paid to care

for your patients. Such uncompassionate
behaviour! Call yourself a nurse?
Too posh to wash?' The rat-tat-tat
reached a climax, then the morse
stopped dead: 'I don't know which is worse,

you who complain or patients who leak
all over my bedclothes.' 'I don't understand.
This is inhuman.' The bird shrieked, 'Look!
What can I do? No hands, no hands!
My job's to keep the patients awake

so there's no dying, not on my floor.
Who cares for me? I don't give a toss –
the pain of others is a total bore.'
A flock of nurses arrived en masse
and the ward was mobbed by birds of distress.

*

Maris turned and crashed into the arms
of a handsome doctor who, very smooth,
swept her into the Relatives' Room,
away from Ludlow. She felt instantly soothed
by his bedroom voice and glistening teeth,

so white they emitted a starry 'Ping!'
whenever he smiled. He was TV-handsome
and Maris felt herself drawn deeply in
to hypnotic eyes. He seemed so winsome
that she felt total confidence in him.

He was speaking, but she had to rouse
herself from looking at his curious suit,
it glittered. She tugged at her crumpled blouse.
'With your husband, I feel we should go the route
of somatic therapy. It wouldn't be right

to be too literal... Doctoring's really theatrical,
medicine's mainly 'On with the show!'
Take Kylie Minogue—what a sporting girl!
What glitz! The fishnets, the feather boa!
She pouted her collagened lips at cancer

danced it away. Yes, Jung was right,
the gods have transformed into diseases
and prey on us daily. We must expiate
our crimes, and see what each deity says
in response to our begging. We have devices

for augury, sacrifice.' 'We're no celebrity
couple, but I'll do anything
to help my husband. We're ordinary,
don't ask me to act or recite or sing,
I can't.' 'It's all about positivity.

Let's cut to the chase. What did he do wrong,
to get the cancer?' 'I don't understand…'
'He must have done something awful to bring
this illness on himself, must have sinned.
Was it resentment? Was it love unbound

by the usual limits? Or was it fear
of relationships? Rage at someone?
His mother? You need to help me here,
give me a clue – half the fun
is working out what a person's done

to earn bad karma.' 'He's not to blame
for having cancer. The man is ill,
not wicked. What's this, a sickening game?'
The doctor came closer. 'I want to heal,'
he whispered, 'and that means the soul

before the body. Will you sign
this consent form on your husband's behalf?
Or are you content to stand there and whine?
We need to operate. My highly-trained staff
are scrubbed up, ready. I've seen enough!

This case is urgent. Here's the form.
Signature here and here and... here.
Let's start this play and perform
the procedure!' And with a flourish the theatre
lit up. Huge shadow-free spotlights flared

to a fanfare of trumpets. In rolled a gurney
bearing Hardy, wheeled by a cast
of dancing nurses. 'Our hierarchy
is an ancient order. I am the last
of the druid-surgeons, I am classed

as god-like so my gown is gold,
not green like my servants. My task, I believe,
is to master the demon that's been so bold
as to conquer this person, command it to leave,
so that this chastened patient may live

to pay tribute to the expanding cult
of Mysterious Bodies. Give me my sword.
Let the ritual start. This man's guilt
is his problem. With my dazzling word
I'll undo his illness. Let him be cured!'

Maris rushed forward, found she was held
by green-robed minions. 'Are you mad?
Why are those frightening nurses veiled?
Why shouldn't a man be furious, then sad,
about his illness?' 'I forbid,' thundered the druid,

'negativity.' He made to plunge
his sword into the heart. 'He must vibrate
to higher frequencies.' Then Maris lunged
at the doctor, scattering initiates.
'Kill me, then,' she screamed, 'because I hate

his cancer. And you're a bunch of fakes
and charlatans.' She overturned a tray
of instruments. 'You're nothing like
a real doctor. This isn't *Peace*, it's a fantasy
of mind over matter. I want reality,

not props and magic.' 'Take him away!'
commanded the druid, then mocked, 'Go ahead!
The evil inside you will have its day.
Your husband, bitch, is as good as dead.'
Maris charged at him. He fled.

BOOK 3

Open the bones, and you shall nothing find
In the best *face* but *filth*, when, Lord, in thee
The *beauty* lies, in the *discovery*.

GEORGE HERBERT

Health isn't making everybody into a Greek
ideal; it's living out the destiny of the body.

ROBERTSON DAVIES

The second door she chose was '*Love*'.
Maris muttered: 'I hope this one's better
than *Peace*.' 'At least we know he's still alive,'
said Wilson, leaning into her
as greyhounds do, for comfort. A corridor

stretched out ahead of them. Two parallel lines
led to infinity. You know the kind:
my father walked them daily last time
he was in for surgery. It soothed his mind
to pace, pyjama'd, through the lanes

of lonely chairs. He wandered the hospital
as, on a supply ship in the Second World War,
he'd tread the length of the starboard fo'csle,
then back down the port, in heavy weather –
thirty paces that stretched even further,

one mile, then two. Now ill, he wouldn't lie down
but persisted in travelling outward,
exploring in his dressing-gown.
He's a ghost in this poem. Not another word.
I'll escort him gently back to his ward.

They walked for ages. 'What the heck?'
asked Wilson, sniffing the corridor's air,
twitching his nostrils. A greyhound can detect
scents a hundred million times better
than us. On Maris, he could scent fear,

her time of the month, exactly how
Hardy had kissed her, a hint of adrenaline.
Then the odour hit her: 'Wow!
What *is* that?' Imagine meat rotting,
pork in a plastic bag, left sweating

out in the heat of a midday sun.
She swallowed, regretted it. A bee
followed the whiff of carrion
in through a door. The reek of ripe poultry
grew stronger. 'Come in! It's only me!'

a weak voice cried. The stench grew worse
as they entered, so they could barely see
for revulsion. 'I've been buzzing the nurse,'
said a man in bed, 'but nobody
comes.' He saw their faces. 'I'm sorry.

I know it's awful. I smell so foul
no one can stand it. Open the window,
it helps. Please don't leave. I feel
so lonely.' His head fell back on the pillow,
huge eyes watching to see if they'd go,

pleading for contact. 'Of course we'll stay,'
said Maris, forcing herself to move
closer. She had to turn away
to hide her gagging, as a stronger wave
of decay washed over her, scent of the grave.

'My name is Phil. I was in the garden
weeding, putting leaves on the fire,
when I felt a stab, like the prick of a thorn
in my ankle tendon. I carried on,
thought nothing of it. But a bacterium,

Clostridium, had entered the sore,
which festered. Now I'm an invalid
but, worse, I'm a social pariah,
a leper who stinks. A man who's putrid
is hard to pity. I wash but I'm always fetid,

I disgust myself, so I can hardly blame
others for leaving.' She wanted to flee
this man who was beginning to drown
in the poisons of his own body.
Maris forced herself closer. His hand was chilly

but he wept when she touched him. 'Don't start!'
she blustered. 'Besides, you're not so bad.
Have you ever smelt a greyhound's fart?
That's awful.' Wilson bridled and glared
with mock offence. She sat on the bed.

'My full name is Philoctetes –
Greek, no fun in school but, still,
it forces you to deal with bullies.'
'He was the archer in the *Iliad*
the one by whose arrow Troy finally fell.'

'That's right. I feel this wound is an eye,'
said Philoctetes. 'It's started to stare
through me, it sees things differently.
At night, when I try to sleep, it flares,
insistent, it throbs, hot as a pulsar

in my body's darkness. It leads the way
inwards and downwards, taking me somewhere
I don't want to go. Some experts say
such an injury knits better
if you keep it open.' 'Isn't cancer

a kind of wound that won't heal?'
asked Maris, dreamily. 'Its luscious lips
speak to me softly,' continued Phil,
'they tell such stories and want me to kiss
a monster...' 'I think you're delirious,'

said Maris. But Phil continued, 'It tears
at me, I'm in a dragon's maw,
infection feeds on me and I can't bear
its breath any longer.' Philoctetes tore
at his filthy dressings. Maris swore.

Where were the nurses? And Ludlow? 'Please,
Won't you help me?' he begged. 'I've got to see
what's happening.' His febrile eyes
were desperate. 'Don't look at me,
said Maris, 'I'm squeamish.' Wilson snapped at a bee

that had landed on the sour bandages.
With care, the greyhound started to gnaw
at the tape that held them. 'I did First Aid
in Brownies,' said Maris and began to tear
at the complex plasters which fell to the floor

like shavings, leaving a pus-stained gauze
pressed to the injury. She felt sick
to see malodorous liquid ooze
from the well of Phil's body. The tissue was stuck
on the scab so Wilson continuously licked,

using his spittle to soak it free
of the crud that covered it. He peeled
it back with infinite patience and, oh so gently,
she pulled off the pad to reveal:
a gaping cave of flesh. Appalled,

Maris stared. In the bloody mess
maggots writhed and she could see bone,
exposed and sticky. She started to retch.
But calmly Wilson said: 'This looks clean,
they've eaten the rotten meat. Maggots' hygiene

is always impeccable.' He lapped
at the larvae, knocking them clear
of the patient. Maris flipped.
'I'd no idea that choosing this door
would feel so awful, like disaster.

She complained, 'I expected that *Love*,'
would be agreeable. It hurts, this ache
of absence, the worry.' 'But you feel alive?'
asked Phil. 'I do. My heart will break,
is breaking.' 'Maris, it's only fake

love that's pretty, pink and fluffy.
True love goes against the grain
of everything easy, and misery
at another's suffering is a sign
of real loving. It can feel like pain,

but only unselfishness can heal
and it stings.' Maris hated this, began
to cry. 'Look at you with a hole
in your foot, all septic. You frighten
us all.' But the suffering man

embraced her. Sometimes, the only grace
we have is to comfort those who hurt less
than we do. Now tears poured down Maris's face
as she, ashamed, felt the dying man bless
her search for Hardy. I must confess

this is strange but, like a shower
of rain, the droplets went
into his wound and soothed the gore
and suddenly the heady scent
of soil after drought, so fresh and fragrant,

spread through the room. Think of the rain
which healed the lepers in *Ben Hur*,
that downpour which washed them to health again.
So, in a side ward, through Maris's despair,
something was happening – I hardly dare

tell you – but Philoctetes's wound
was closing. Just then a large bald head
poked round the door. 'Help! If they find
me here, I'm as good as dead.'
'Who's after you?' asked Maris. 'I'm Ichabod,'

he laughed but suddenly withdrew
as the sound of a baying hunting pack
grew closer, howling with rage. They heard
urgent voices: 'He must have doubled back
past X-Ray, along Cardiac

Corridor. There! I can see his trail
of dirty footsteps!' The lynch mob cried
for the blood of the filthy criminal
who should not live. Horrified,
Maris and Wilson rushed outside

to see the source of such violence.
Deserted. First they followed the sound
down passages till they lost all sense
of direction. This is where a greyhound
is very handy. Nose to the ground,

he followed the rabble's curious scent
to the entrance of a classical temple.
It had an impressive pediment
with gods and goddesses, Corinthian capitals
and columns – not common in a hospital.

They stood to admire the building's frieze
which depicted the eternal fight
of heroic flesh with monstrous disease.
Warriors flexed their muscles to fight
chimeras that were forced to submit.

An imposing sign said: *The Body Museum.*
They looked at each other and went inside,
past a monument to the Opposable Thumb,
DNA jewellery, which Maris eyed
uneasily. 'I can't see anywhere to hide,

can you?' she said. 'By their odour
I know they're here.' So they entered the Hall
of the Body Beautiful, where the full repertoire
of physical glory was ranged on pedestals:
the David, a Perseus, the Dying Gaul,

a goddess Diana – celebrities
of the ancient torso, all flexed and trim,
designed to be seen. Unpainted eyes
were blank, moon-abstract. It was a gym
of superlatives, idealised limbs

in the throes of passion, victory or youth.
Maris felt a growing disquiet
here, where all was Beauty and Truth,
no oozing wounds, no bouquet of blood and shit.
It was cold and inhuman. 'Wait a minute...'

She stopped by one statue. 'This one's different.'
And, sure enough, this figure was fleshy.
His limbs were flushed with a healthy pigment
that gave his form a sheen of rosy
well-being, he was so vibrant and sexy

that Maris wanted to kiss his skin
just for the fragrant, silky feel of it.
This statue was the kind of man
you'd want to have children by, you'd fall at his feet
and he'd adore you, because he's complete

in himself and has no hidden agenda,
no neediness, no taking hostage,
but joy in your body, the way you are.
This statue was frank and returned her gaze
as her equal. 'It's Ichabod!' she said. Unfazed

he winked, not unlike Captain Jean-Luc Picard,
full of intelligence tinged with mirth,
which is very attractive. The man is hard
but knows how not to be. I have great faith
in people who've understood their own worth

but don't have to prove it. 'Hello Maris, my dear,
I've been hoping you'd find me. Don't look now
but those silly statues are inching closer.
And, sure enough, a Venus de Milo
was bearing down on them. 'How much do you know

about me, then, darling?' 'What do you mean?
You're a stranger.' 'Maris, are you sure?'
She eyed a sinister Laocoön
who was edging towards them. 'How's the wear and tear
on your cruciate ligament? You see, I am aware

of that migraine you're fighting, and the twinge
in your ovaries, your period is due.'
'How could you know?' 'I savour every change
in our body. In fact, you'll find I get you
better than you do yourself.' Now statues

40

surrounded them in a tight formation,
bold and menacing. 'I am your mentor,'
said Ichabod, 'a kind of incarnation.
My job is to show you what the body's for.
It has its wisdom. And now, for my floor

show.' He proceeds to demonstrate
the endocrine system and its diseases.
With arteries, he delineates
atherosclerosis, then *diabetes
mellitus*, what happens to the testes

in untreated cases of gonorrhoea,
then pustules, chancres, herpetic lesions.
This display provoked a roar of horror
from the statues, outraged that Medical Illustration
had lowered the tone of their hallowed museum.

They howled. 'We like the body apart,
single and separate. Not leaving a trail
of cells behind it. We're works of art
and this creature should be put on trial
for being offensive. It's an animal!'

'Watch it,' growled Wilson, going eye to eye
with a marble greyhound which lost the stare
between them. Wilson was mollified.
Something flashed. A migraine aura,
giving Maris the germ of an idea,

a way of escaping. 'Wilson, come here.
Ichabod, how do statues behave
when lights are strobing?' 'A sculpture
can't resist posing.' 'So we could deceive
them with lighting, use it to leave?'

'Excellent plan!' Maris turned and attacked:
'Is there no honour among sculptures?
Let Ichabod have his say, stand back!
Call yourself ancients? Let's see his figure
once and for all. That would be fair.'

The statues muttered but reluctantly froze
in attentive postures. Ichabod stood
on his podium, began to metamorphose
into something wondrous. The crowd
gasped in horror as he showed

himself. He said, 'The body's a dream.
Each step we take is a separate flare
into darkness.' Suddenly Ichabod flamed
with a radiance like an opening door.
He lifted Maris into the fire

that played on him now like a waterfall
of streaming vitality that rose like heat
from them together. Forget the soul,
the body itself is so complete
it needs no guidance. For all that it's dirt,

soul follows it. Maris felt her sight
sharpen. He said: 'You are my eyes
into matter. My anchor, my delight,
my sentient hell, but I also recognise
you are my partner and my paradise.'

She laughed with joy, along with Ichabod
and, as they talked, the flames died down.
Maris felt suddenly very sad,
not knowing why. They stood there plain,
facing each other. Then a menacing line

of statues grabbed them. 'I've seen enough
of this impiety.' A Hercules
manhandled Maris. 'Time to get tough,'
he roared and knocked her to her knees.
'There's only one way to guarantee

their compliance. We'll have to cast
them both as statues. He's been told,
but he won't listen.' Things happened fast
now. Cupid and Psyche blindfolded
the couple, and they were pulled

towards a workshop. 'You know, the feet
of some Greek statues which have survived
show that the soles were bearing weight.
That means the figures were cast alive
in molten metal,' said a Nubian slave,

pushing them roughly. 'It should only hurt
for a second, then you'll be like us,
smooth and immortal!' 'You perverts!'
screamed Maris. 'Don't talk to Zeus
like that!' A Hermes hit her. 'We need to discuss...'

Suddenly a voice cried, 'Freeze!
I want you all to hold that pose,
look at the camera and say "Cheese!"'
A flash. And the statues re-composed
themselves. 'That's lovely, darlings. But lose

the humans.' The photographer's voice
commanded, 'Don't you think that flesh
looks dull by bronze? Venus! More poise
from you!' He blinded them with flash.
Maris and Ichabod made a dash

for the door where Wilson stood, his paw
on the light switch. 'That was great!'
he continued. 'Just a couple more...
And try to look very intimate
with the camera, sweethearts.' 'Wilson, we'll wait

outside. Be careful.' Hand in hand
they escaped. Maris felt suddenly very shy.
'That crowd in there is out of its mind
on steroids,' said Bod. Live to fight another day...
You *do* know the body's for giving away,

don't you?' 'That doesn't sound like fun,'
said Maris. 'Don't worry, we'll do what we can
before that happens.' With that Wilson
tore past at full tilt, a murderous din
behind him. 'The vogueing's over!' he said. They ran.

BOOK 4

Headed like a snake
Necked like a drake
Backed like a beam
Tailed like a rat
Footed like a cat.

Greyhound
BOOK OF ST ALBANS

I'm the one who has the body,
you're the one who holds the breath.

You know the secret of my body,
I know the secret of your breath.

DĒVARA DĀSIMAYYA

A sluice room. Silence. Then a terrible whiff.
'Wilson! You didn't!' 'Reaction to stress.
Sorry. Can't help it. It's just relief.'
'Phew!' said Ichabod. 'Control your arse
or they'll find us all dead. I heard them pass,

but I think it would be wise to wait
a little longer. Maris, please explain
the greyhound. Here boy, sit!'
Wilson bristled. 'If you want to retain
your goolies, you shifty shit-for-brains,

show some respect! Don't forget,
a wolf was my forebear and your jugular vein
is plainly visible.' 'Now, calm yourself,'
soothed Maris, 'he didn't mean
to insult you. But neither of us has seen

a talking dog before.' 'I'm no pet.
I'm the last of a noble line
of greyhounds which are so fleet of foot
it's said that we can outrun time.
So that you know, my real name

is Zoltán Mistlove Sirius. My pedigree
is ancient. It was my ancestors
who hunted in the *Mabinogi*,
quick as sea-swifts before my master,
Lord of the Otherworld. I never tire

of chasing the nimble. It's me who visits
widows in darkness on their sleepless beds,
when grief's at its most exquisite.
Their hands always find my velvet head.
We never speak, but they're comforted.

I followed Tobias from his father's house
when he went with the angel. I fed St. Roque
when he had the plague and couldn't rouse
himself. I helped him to walk
and kept him cheerful. I only talk

to those who're being hunted by death
and are aware of it. I fall and rise,
impersonal but close as breath.
In the dark I am the only eyes
that see because you can never lie

to a dog.' 'So why the name Wilson?'
'A cartoon athlete – "Wilson of the *Wizard*".
Like me, a sporting superman
dressed in a sleek black leotard.
He lived on the moor, broke all records,

like racing a train, which he easily beat.
It was he who perfected the Fosbury Flop.
He swam the Channel – all kinds of feats,
was a fighter pilot.' Ichabod began to clap
sarcastically. 'I don't know how you cope

with all your achievements.' Maris looked shocked.
Wilson snapped back. 'At least I know
what I am. I'm not some shallow jock
who alters with who I'm talking to.
Look at you, Ichabod, you're changing now!

Your skin is sprouting a greyhound's pelt!'
'Don't mock me, Rover, it's involuntary.
Tell me, have you never felt
yourself mimic someone? It's sympathy.'
'To me it looks untrustworthy.

I'm a dog of principle. I believe in foundation,
the basic rhythm of in and out,
breath under everything, inspiration!
I'm no flibbertigibbet gadabout
like you.' And Wilson stuck his snout

into Ichabod's crotch. 'You filthy mutt!'
Wilson snorted, 'Flirting's all very well
if you're flighty.' 'Get off my foot!'
Their fighting made Maris tearful.
'Is it true,' she asked, 'that dogs can smell

cancer on people?' She began to cry.
Remorseful, Wilson and Ichabod stood by,
helpless. 'You're my friends, and I can't take sides
when you bicker.' Ichabod looked suddenly nude.
'The truth is I'm lost, and I haven't a clue

how to go about finding my husband'.
She sobbed like a child, hiccupped for air.
Wilson licked the back of her hand,
and Maris was grateful. Suddenly the door
was flung open by a starchy sister.

'You should have been here an hour ago,'
she thundered. The annual Deep Clean
has started. 'Where do you want us to go?'
asked Ichbod swiftly, sounding keen.
'Follow me! We're way down in the hygiene

tables and the Infection Police
are due to visit. Patients are getting sick
from superbugs. I want to see my face
in this floor. Work fast and think cosmetic.
When you've mopped perhaps the dog can lick

all surfaces, but don't let anybody see
him doing it. I want a sheen
on everything. Thank God for the agency,
cleaners on staff take too much time
doing a proper job. A superficial shine

will do. Now that you've started I
can go for a break.' 'That woman's a scandal,'
said Maris. From the corner of her eye
something scuttled. 'This place should be sterile...'
'Oh my God, it's a Microbe's Ball,'

shouted Ichabod. 'It's rare, we're in for a real treat.
Wilson, how's your bossa nova?
The last ball left me out on my feet,
with a week-long toxin hangover.
Look, if we're quick we can follow her!'

A group went by in fancy dress and masks
of the most flamboyant carnival style,
some wearing hats. They were grotesques,
some faces covered in shimmering veils
made of unfamiliar textiles.

Ichabod began to sing, 'I'm in the mood
for dancin'!' 'I told you he's shallow,'
said Wilson. 'I'm not being rude
but that's embarrassing.' 'We'll be fine if we keep a low
profile.' 'Fat chance of *that* with *him* in tow,'

muttered Wilson. But when they entered the ballroom
he looked around with unaffected awe
at the crowds, sniffed the exotic perfume
of creatures he'd never smelt the like before:
day-glo couples waltzed round the stairs,

jolly *Bordetella pertussis* in red,
a *Trypanosoma* being pursued
by a *Naegleria fowleri* whose monstrous head
threatened to eat it. A proud
Staphylococcus aureus split with a loud

pop. Maris saw Ludlow. 'Yoo-hoo, over here!'
And she waved like mad until he came.
'Ah Maris, Wilson, there you are!
I thought I'd lost you, my lovely dame.
Isn't this splendid? There are famous

fighters here. Are you all right,
Maris? You're looking quite pale.'
And Maris, who had been feeling faint
and wobbly sat down. 'Have you eaten at all
since I last saw you? No wonder you feel ill.'

'But I swore to fast till Hardy was here.'
'If you weaken you'll be of no use
to him. I think you're being a martyr.
Microbe cuisine is very nutritious,
their cheeses especially delicious.'

'I couldn't,' said Maris, with her knees
held tightly together. 'I could never forget
that we're surrounded by enemies.'
'Where?' asked Ludlow. 'You mean these parasites?
Never. There are lots of lymphocytes

around to protect you.' 'Don't be a puritan,'
Ichabod joined in. 'I'm surprised
at you. I'm friends with hosts of pathogens
and so are you, if only you realised.
But microbes have always been demonised.'

'Ah!' said Ludlow. 'I'm called to the lists.
The body's a party, we're here to enjoy
the fiesta. See you after the joust.
I know this germ and I'll be very annoyed
if I can't unseat the silly cowboy,

tally ho!' And suddenly the herald
tapped the mike and asked, 'Can you all hear?'
'Yes!' cried the crowd. Dressed in brocade
with sequins, he bowed. 'Put your hands together,
ladies and gents, for our guests of honour.

First, the bacteria: *Streptococci*!'
(I'll translate as we go. Dental decay,
sore throats.) '*Mycobacteria*!'
(Tuberculosis and leprosy.) 'Pray
stand for *Shigella*!' (Dysentery.)

'And the *Vibrios*!' (That's cholera.)
Some came in rods, some in coils, some spherical.
'Let's hear it for *Treponema* and *Chlamydia*!'
(So many of them sound lyrical
till you see what they do to a testicle.)

Next the viruses. He called *Varicella zoster*
(Chickenpox, shingles.) Viral lifestyles
are violent, they can behave like bruisers.
Some, like Rambo, burst through cell walls
and people, like the dreaded *Ebola*.

Then came the moulds and in pride of place
the fungi – with *Candida*
all in white. Then protozoa – the horrible face
of *Giardia lamblia*. Next, the algae
and Maris remembered lithe *Spirogyra*

from school and clapped. *Penicillium*
(a mould) came with the prions, all out of order
but pushed his way to the front like a bum
but the microbes just laughed. 'And here,'
shouted the herald, 'is Debutante of the Year:

the Bluetongue virus! And she's wearing a gown
made by her mother.' She looked so demure –
bashful, she kept her shy gaze down.
'Gorgeous, isn't she? Causing quite a stir!
This lovely can kill a sheep in three hours.'

'That's nothing to boast about,' Maris scolded.
Bod replied, 'Microbes don't make us ill,
it's the body's reaction which gives us the cold.
Diphtheria only ever kills
if it's sick itself.' The herald again: 'Final call

for the priest who's due to officiate
at the lichen wedding. I can confirm
a doctor will kindly demonstrate
how to extract a five-metre tapeworm
without it or the patient coming to harm.

Yes, madam, you roll it on a stick.'
Maris squirmed. She looked around.
She'd never seen a crowd more antic
or lively. Germs you'd hate to find in a wound
were twirling in wildly extravagant gowns.

Old friends met, 'This is my fiancée.'
Kiss, kiss. 'You're looking very well!'
she heard one fuzzy spore say
to a virus. 'Thanks. Seen any good cells
lately?' 'No, I think they're going downhill.'

Imagine a disco painted by Bosch –
microbes are social animals
and they crowded together in such a crush
they looked like a seething carousel
pulsing with life. 'And last of all,'

announced the herald, 'I propose a toast…'
'They're nothing but a bunch of chavs,'
said Maris. '…To the humans. I give you: Our Hosts!
'That's us being honoured, stand up and wave!'
and the spotlight found them. Slightly unnerved

Maris blinked in the light and swiftly bobbed.
She was applauded by a roaring sea
of germs. 'You're such a snob,'
continued Ichabod, 'don't you love their joy
in association?' 'You're quite the playboy,

aren't you?' teased Maris. 'You're not bad yourself,'
and he pulled her on to the dance floor.
'This isn't low-life, it's ourselves
we're seeing. Look at that flair!
I think that spore with the green hair

fancies you.' On a tiny stage
a germ performed a fierce flamenco,
a fight with a deadly bacteriophage.
A queue formed for the bucking bronco.
'If you don't mind, Bod, I think I'll go

to look at the buffet.' There were yoghurts and agars,
miso, elderflower champagne,
cider and seventeen different kinds of beer.
The waiter pressed her. Maris looked pained.
'All right, just to please you, I'll taste the wine

and, to go with it, a transparent sliver
of that.' 'Madam, it's vintage Stilton.'
The waiter piled a plate high for her.
The cheese was so ripe he needed a spoon
to serve it. Maris ate all the crumbs

and went for seconds. It tasted of sweat
and sexual bodies. Another glass
and the world looked better. She soon forgot
her vow to fast, had to confess
she was hungry. She met a friendly virus

in the line for pudding. More drink, and he began
to look attractive and rather tasty.
'I'm sorry, I didn't quite catch your name,'
said Maris. A bunch of celebrity
microbes passed, it set the paparazzi

flashing. First, arrogant, came HIV.
Maris's new friend pushed against her, hard
and whispered his name. 'I've heard of you vaguely,
Papillomavirus.' He pressed his business card
into her hand. Then, under armed guard

came smallpox, followed by SARS
(the *Corona* virus). Maris's would-be beau
moved closer in and took her arm
as a deafening calypso
marked the start of the fashion show.

First, *Rotavirus* in metallic gold
swayed her way down the catwalk
waving and smiling. The crowd went wild
to see her swishing her spectacular cloak,
bristling with rows of tiny spikes

to open her victim, like cunning keys.
Next came anthrax, wearing polka dots
in pink and black matching accessories.
Papilloma came closer. 'You're a sexpot,
I'll bet. Why don't we two split?

I know a very colourful bar.'
'The models you see are on the List
of Best-Dressed Microbes for this year!'
Maris felt Wilson nudge her wrist,
looking concerned. 'Don't be a pest!'

'Maris, you need to lay off the booze.'
'Wilson, look at that haute couture...'
'You've got much more than you think to lose,'
persisted the dog. But the allure
of her novel companion and his care

for her was making Maris feel rash.
'If ever a virus was dressed to kill,
it's him,' hissed Wilson. But such panache
had turned her head. *C. difficile*
strode down the catwalk in eau-de-nil.

'Evolution is fashion. Flounces and frills
are our future! Camouflage
is *the* look to wear in a hospital.'
Headstrong *MRSA* and her entourage,
came next, each sporting a décolletage

to die for. We're all clothed in bacteria,
a lingerie made of netting and lace
more delicate than any Marks & Spencer
can provide. You've never seen my face
without its flora. Wilson raced

over to Ludlow. 'And now, the queen
of viruses! My favourite and yours: Influenza!'
Wilson to Ludlow: 'A virus with onco-genes,
is courting Maris.' 'It causes cancer.
I can smell him. We need to stop her.'

Papilloma was whispering sweet nothings.
'You're posh. I'm not. Let's have some fun...
I was in a gang but now I'm going
straight. My street name was Venomous, I was mean,
carrying knives and illegal guns.

Ludlow shook her. 'That's quite enough.
We're leaving.' Maris protested. 'But I'm all right.'
'You've got to trust me. Your piece of rough
is an opportunistic parasite,
I've called Immunity and phagocytes

are coming.' Whistles, sirens. All hell broke loose:
and hosts of T- and B- and natural killer cells
like a squadron of the SAS
abseiled from the ceiling, deploying molecules.
In seconds, no microbes were left in the hall.

BOOK 5

We do not *become* ill: we *are* ill.

THORWALD DETHLEFSEN

Anyone can talk to a sick person, but a medicine man alone, through his medicine, can address a disease.

RICHARD GROSSINGER

I've said already that I won't feel well
till this poem's finished and I find what I mean
about health and loving. It's a hospital,
this place I'm constructing line by line,
with clinics in it and sunlit rooms

open to anyone. Words are my health,
the struggle to hear and transcribe the tune
behind what I'm given by word of mouth,
it's the only work that can make me immune
to lying. May my language gene

grant me haemoglobin and many platelets,
potency deep inside bone marrow.
My safety lies with other poets
who've shown the way they took through shadows.
Milton, Villon, be with me now.

I want to capture what it is to care
for someone you love who's very ill,
how quickly you age as you see them suffer,
you'd do anything to make them well,
but you can't. Now help me, Virgil,

give me the strength of your long sinews
to capture that brave but painful smile
couples exchange when they both know
the score. Help me to draw on wells
that are clean and kind and plentiful.

What do you say when someone you love
is dying and there's nothing you can do
to stop it happening, and you're alive
and well, nowhere near through
adoring them, and you can't follow?

One body's never enough. My reach
is long. Of one thing you can be sure
I'll never give up on this endless search
for you and it's my only cure,
to touch you. Yes, stranger, I mean you.

*

'What *is* it with bees in this place? They're everywhere!'
said Maris as they walked, subdued
down a long, deserted corridor.
'There's a line of them looking for food,
can't think what they find. Don't be in a mood

with me, Wilson. It turned out all right.'
The greyhound answered, 'What I'd like to know
is why Ichabod was out of sight,
gossiping, no doubt, and dancing disco
just when you needed him.' 'Let it go,

Lassie, you heard what she said.'
Ichabod watched a bee on his hand.
'Right now I'm much more interested
in finding breakfast.' Then he turned,
playing the air guitar. 'If you don't understand,

why don't you go back to being a wolf
and leave us to it?' 'Why, you bimbo,
you good-for-nothing, deviant elf,
say that again!' 'That's it, Paddy Paws,
attack, if it helps you to ignore

your own shortcomings.' But even their usual spat
lacked energy, as the passage walls
made the liveliest insult fall strangely flat.
They glared at each other but, in a while,
both tired of being puerile

and walked in silence. 'This feels all wrong,'
said Ludlow, 'but I don't know why.'
Ichabod started to whistle a song
but stopped. 'There's something wild,
a presence I can't identify...'

Along the ventilation ducts
above them they heard a reptilian skitter
as if it were a conduit for rats
escaping a larger predator.
'What is there for them to eat up there?'

Maris wondered. Ludlow answered. 'Rats survived
on Brylcreem sucked from soldiers' hair
in World War One and they've evolved
to live on electric wiring.' Wilson sniffed the air,
every muscle alert to danger

and the further they walked, the more oppressive
the passage became. It was like that hour
at dusk when objects come alive,
a pagan time, when you feel the pressure
of something other on the atmosphere.

It's panic, it turns your bowels to water.
Maris was sweating. Suddenly a creature on wings
hurtled towards her, caught in her hair.
She screamed at its hysterical flapping.
Its claws drew blood. Ludlow flung

the beast away from her. It flew,
ungainly, misshapen, out of sight.
'What was that? A rabid cuckoo?'
Ludlow shuddered. 'I think it might
be a heart attack tracking live meat

to lodge in. 'You mean, we're being hunted
by illnesses?' 'Could be, but I feel there's more
to this place.' They looked with dread
at each other and an atavistic fear
made Wilson bristle. He thought he saw

a feral flicker so, instinctively, the sight
hound gave chase and snapped the creature's neck.
It was a proliferating leukocyte,
small but vicious. But when he turned to go back
he felt himself come under attack

from inside himself. He wanted to kill
everything he had become.
He despised himself for being docile,
a pet, a poodle, a killer tamed.
All the instincts that he'd overcome

revolted. He raised his head and howled
with desolation, called for his kind,
his irises gold as the eyes of wolves
who hate the haunts of humankind.
'Wilson, be quiet. Are you out of your mind?'

asked Maris but she quickly froze
when she saw a salivating cur
where Wilson had stood. His hackles rose.
Fear coarsened every inch of his fur.
If she moved, she knew, he would savage her.

I heard of a woman who'd been so sick
her smell had changed. She was now an intruder
to her dog. She expected a welcome of licks
and loving. He turned aggressor,
so savage she scarcely recovered.

Maris spoke. He watched her throat,
frothing. Human words fell
like stones around him, a further threat
and, foaming now, his black lips curled,
revealing his fangs. The mad hound snarled

so, to soothe him, she began to sing
about the dog that was her companion:
'Sirius, bright star of evening,
he who daily outsprints the sun,
leaves in the dust a thousand trillion

planets. Sweet Sirius, the blaze
on a greyhound's flank. He shines
nightly so that I may gaze
on him, my celestial chaperone.
While I breathe we're never alone.'

She looked and the wolf had lain down,
was Wilson again, so Maris flung
herself on her friend. He whined,
appalled at what he'd nearly done.
'Jesus! That was just like *White Fang*,'

said Ichabod. 'No, stupid, *Call of the Wild*
when Buck went native and became a wolf.'
Said Ludlow, 'That was *lupus*.' The doctor eyed
Wilson. 'The body attacks itself
with all its weapons, in the belief

it's fighting an enemy. *Horror autoxicus*,
lack of self-tolerance, friendly fire,
and I think it could happen to any of us.'
'You mean our defences are going haywire?'
asked Maris. 'That's my worst nightmare,'

said Ludlow. 'What's happening to my hands?'
He held them up and his fingers were bent
like blackthorn buckled by mountain winds.
So twisted were his knuckle joints,
they looked like the top of a stick. 'It's time we went.

Rheumatoid arthritis.' 'Look at this,'
said Ichabod, with sudden terror,
a spot like the blotch on sycamore
leaves appeared. Through thick conjunctivitis
he knew what it was: Kaposi's sarcoma.

'The purple badge of HIV,'
Ludlow said tersely. 'No time to lose.'
He turned, but Maris's internal eyes
saw her fronded capillaries
swamped by tumours, her arteries

flowing with mud. 'Leukaemia,'
said Ludlow observing a bruise
spread on her leg. 'Or septicaemia.
If we don't escape, this whole enterprise
is doomed.' Ichabod sat down to snooze

but Wilson softly nudged him awake.
'Come on, Travolta, we've got to go!'
For each step forward, they seemed to take
two back. 'It's this passage,' said Ludlow,
'the progress we're making is far too slow

for all this effort.' So they trekked some more,
caught in a storm of gravity,
only to see the threshold withdraw
even further. With redoubled energy
they slogged, but it was infinity

to cross and they could never arrive.
Ludlow muttered, 'At this pace,
we'll never get out of here alive.
Something's happened to time and space.'
'If you like,' said Wilson, 'I could try to race

whatever it is. My line of greyhound
was bred in order to take on time.
Besides, I'd like to make amends
for earlier. Six hundred years old and I'm
considered to be in my coursing prime.'

The corridor squelched, seemed to elongate
ever further. Now Ludlow felt its raptor eye
focus on them and concentrate
with terrible purpose. Ludlow thought: 'We're prey.
If we do nothing we're going to die

from the inside out.' Nonchalant
at first, Wilson trotted, getting a feel
for the dimensions of the present.
His muscles rippled, smooth as oil,
measuring distance. Then he uncoiled

himself sleekly, like a metal spring,
and took off running, as if the hare
of seconds sped ahead of him, jinking.
Have you ever seen people stop to admire
a greyhound as it changes gear

to chase? The thrill of seeing perfect design
rejoice in its purpose, which is elegant speed,
even the tearing greyhound grins
with pleasure, feeling suddenly freed
from weight (small creatures, be very afraid).

Coursing now, Wilson made a bee-line
for the entrance, which didn't seem so far.
He set himself in the fastest lane
in a racecourse made of singing air,
running low like a jaguar.

Through the space-time continuum he flew,
stepping so lightly he left no prints.
He hunched together and, like a kangaroo,
his hind legs overtook the front
and now it was he started to sprint.

All around him, it was snowing stars
and through his skin they could see the veins
of nebulae as bright elsewheres
hurtled towards them. Wilson gained
on his goal but now the supernatural strain

was showing. Some say that time expanded heals
and who would not want its ecstasy?
Wilson exceeded his reach and fell
on the exit and, using his quivering body
as a bridge, he let the company

climb out of the self-consuming place
into their past, where they were safe,
at least for the moment. Maris buried her face
in Wilson's withers with renewed belief.
A long time passed before he caught his breath.

'That was Superman saving Lois Lane,'
said Ichabod, 'when he flew around
the planet and made it counter-spin
so he could pull her car from the ground!'
They laughed and relaxed to the sound

of something human. '*En garde!*'
said Maris, who was still uptight.
'That was sneaky, cancer. If you're so hard,
I challenge you now to an open fight
mano a mano, in broad daylight.

You're not having Hardy. I was on the shelf –
the shits I dated! It took an age
to find a good man.' Beside herself
she screamed, 'I've only just got him trained.
This will be my one and only marriage,

hands off!' Ludlow whispered, 'Keep it down!'
but she'd launched into a full-blown *haka*.
'Shush! Enemies listen to every sound.
And while I admire your lack of fear
what you need is an expert tracker

to follow the clues left by the disease.'
Ludlow looked at his straightened hands.
He coughed. 'That *is* my field of expertise.
I told you before. As well as physician
I consider myself a rhetorician.

I address the illness, persuade it to leave
the patient. I learned to track
wild cats back to their nursing caves
with an Aborigine in the outback.
He taught me stillness and all the tricks,

so now I can follow the pungent spore
of ants, can tell you where a mosquito
has landed, or if a doe is mature
by the print of her hoof. I can even show
you cloud-prints.' 'If so, why don't we shadow

Hardy's cancer? If I were her
where would I get my strength? Where would I hide?'
Now Wilson spoke, 'I would go deeper
into this building. I would be a bride
of darkness.' Their newly enthusiastic guide

was scanning the ground for any signs.
The others fell silent. 'Just a minute...'
he said. There was a drop of warm, saline
blood rich, the colour of pomegranate
and, careful not to trample on it,

they began to follow the crimson spoor.
'Each sickness has a totem animal
with its own hungers. And if you care
to learn its language, in a while
you can talk with it.' They followed the trail

and found themselves in front of the door
marked *Death*. 'I didn't want to go this way,'
said Maris grimly. 'If you don't come further,
I'll understand,' she said. The foyer
went cold. Ichabod quipped, 'You could hardly say

that *Love* was fun.' Wilson caught Maris's eye.
They said it all in a silent exchange.
'*Death* may not mean that we have to die,'
said Ludlow, 'it's probably more about change.
I'm in. I want to extend the range

of my tracking and I have a feeling
that this is where I'll learn something new
for medicine.' Maris was past caring
where she went or what she had to do.
She opened the door, led her friends through.

BOOK 6

To wait for one who never comes,
To lie in bed and not to sleep,
To serve well and not to please,
To have a horse that will not go,
To be sick and lack the cure,
To be a prisoner without hope,
To lose the way when you would journey,
To stand at a door that none will open,
To have a friend who would betray you,
These are the ten pains of death.

GIOVANNI FLORIO

They entered a waiting room. From a chair
an anxious-looking woman rose
to meet them. Slight, with sleek black hair,
she seemed distraught and timidly asked, 'Excuse
me, doctor, is there any news

about my child?' They felt instant sympathy.
Such pain you could never fabricate.
'Whatever it is, I want you to tell me.'
Her violet eyes were staring straight
at Ludlow. He thought, 'Concentrate,'

but failed and blushed. His bedside manner
kicked in. 'Sit down, my dear. This isn't my case,
but I'm sure he's receiving excellent care.'
He wanted to stroke her troubled face
but resisted. 'Doctor, do you think he'll race

again? They say he could be world champion.'
She smiled. 'We're a family of athletes.'
And, indeed, she was a pocket Amazon,
shapely and feminine, but with discreet
beauty and an expression so sweet

that they wanted to help, protect her from harm.
Maris sat by her side. 'I know how you feel.'
She placed an understanding arm
around her. 'It drives me wild that Hardy is ill
and I can't heal him. It's such an ordeal.'

The woman blinked. 'But I'm a *mother*.
You have children? No? Then you don't understand.
You can't compare kids with a mere lover,
it's more intense.' She wrung her hands,
'Not like you and your little friend.' 'No, husband,

70

actually.' Wilson bristled
and Maris muttered, 'Don't start again,'
but, undeterred, the greyhound snarled
then barked. She hissed at him, 'You're being a pain!'
'I feel uneasy. Maris, look at those men!'

She turned. Ludlow'd moved, was sitting next
to the woman, listening like her slave,
while Ichabod tried but failed to suppress
a scent of involuntary aftershave –
Eau Sauvage. Wilson barked. 'Behave!'

Maris commanded. 'Never forget,'
he said with a dignity that made her ashamed,
'I love you, but I'm not your pet.
Unless you hold me in higher esteem,'
he continued to Maris's growing alarm,

'I'm warning you that I'll simply leave.
We haven't known each other that long,
why should I be here if you don't believe
my instincts? Somehow this woman's very wrong.
Behind that act she's preternaturally strong,

she spooks me.' 'Wilson, I'm so, so sorry.'
'Whatever she's feeling, it isn't grief,
more...exultation.' Maris eyed
her more wisely. '*She's* no helpless waif,'
said Wilson, 'she's over-brimming with life.'

'But that's attractive,' said Maris. 'Ichabod likes her.'
Wilson sorted, 'That boy's so gullible,
he has the gravitas of a coiffeur.
I can't describe it. I know what I feel,
she's not on the level. Look at him drool,

it's disgusting.' Trying to seem casual,
Ichabod strutted and flexed his pecs.
The mother responded in a little girl
voice. A teenager flirting at a skating rink,
Ichabod's neck had flushed bright pink.

Then he bounced up to Maris. 'Isn't she great?
First time I've met a 'Yummy Mummy'.
Poor woman, she's been in such a state.'
Pheromones squirted in a fine spray
around him. 'Oh boy, what a body!'

The mother's cardigan fell open to show
a cropped top cradling a voluptuous bosom
and a belly so taut it was almost hollow.
Ludlow, too, was clearly overcome,
he simpered. Ichabod resumed

his worship and when an insistent bee
troubled the lady, made a transparent cage
of his hands and set the insect free
out of the window, where it buzzed, in a rage
to get her. Maris felt on edge

and asked, suspiciously. 'How old
are you?' She laughed. '*That* would be telling.
I'm from peasant stock, we're used to the cold.
Our tribe is born to exultant singing
out in the snow. We only bring

up the strong. We live by family values –
early to bed, rise with the lark,
hard work, then games, collective virtues.'
'Whatever they are.' 'Maris, that remark
is beneath you,' said Ludlow. 'We're matriarchs.

My great-great-grandmother's still alive
with all her own teeth and thick, glossy hair.
Left to ourselves, we refuse to die.'
'What does that mean?' asked Maris sharply.
Ichabod hissed at her, 'Jealousy

is *so* unattractive.' 'Time to press on,'
said Maris. But Ichabod and Ludlow preferred
to stay. She tried her best to win their attention
but failed. Enchanted by this perfect mother,
the truth was: they no longer saw her.

'Tell me, my dear, about your husband.'
Now that she'd won the menfolk over,
the woman took Maris aside. 'I don't understand
why you're alone.' 'He has blood cancer,'
said Maris. 'My friend the Administrator

could help you find – is it Hardy? – I'm sure.'
Maris stiffened. 'Don't stand so close.'
'Afraid of our feelings?' the mother purred,
moved so near that the heat of her torso
troubled Maris. The woman glowed

with such a charge of energy
it felt erotic. She stroked Maris's cheek
and kissed her lips ever so lightly,
leaving Maris unable to speak.
Wilson growled, 'You sinister freak!

'You've charmed the others but beware
of me.' He butted the woman out of range.
'I'm watching you,' he warned and stared,
unmoving. Maris felt strange,
as if her aura had been subtly changed.

'Yes, Head Office is just what you need,'
said the mother brightly as the other two
joined them, taking little heed
of the tension, the threatening undertow
to the conversation. 'I can even show

you how to get there by the back way.'
'This Administrator, you know him?'
'Oh yes,' she laughed, 'intimately.
Better, poor love, than he thinks. He's slim,
glasses, full of self-esteem –

you know the type. We have an understanding.'
She winked and slinked her way upstairs.
Ludlow had fallen behind, was examining
a fascinating smudge of glair,
which he sniffed and tasted, like the silver

left by slugs or snails. 'No… it can't be…'
he muttered. 'Is this possibly the creature?
I thought such talk was a made-up story,
I must take samples to be sure…
How terribly exciting!' They knocked the door.

'Watch this!' the woman said with a wicked grin,
'I'll wind him up for a bit of a giggle.'
From inside a business-like voice said, 'Come in!'
Maris overheard, 'You? I thought we had a deal.'
'Relax, my darling. Just a social call.'

'I told you never to visit me here…'
Seeing the others, 'You need an appointment!'
he said, as he hid behind his computer.
'Speaking to people isn't efficient
use of my time.' 'But this is entertainment!'

she cooed. 'Tomorrow's Parking, Bogs and Boilers.
Thursday's Target Prioritisation.
The doctors are spending money like water.
Then Friday I'm writing our Strategic Plan.'
'Darling, we need some information.

I – we – need to find her husband.'
A bead of sweat formed on his upper lip.
His glasses glinted. 'Until he's found
we're going nowhere.' He started to type,
then rearranged his paperclips.

'You have a problem, by the way, with bees,'
chipped in Ichabod. Wilson looked quizzical.
but listened. 'Yes, it's a form of vitality,
something to do with collective cells.
I've tried to destroy them but, so far, I've failed.'

He turned to Maris. 'Fill out the waiting-list quiz
on behalf of your husband. What's his age?
Your name will be entered in the draw for a prize
if you answer wisely. His annual wage?
How many dependants? Does he eat veg?

Has he ever smoked?' Then he fed the paper
into a scanner and put up his feet.
The printer churned and gave a chunder,
spat out: 'Decision: Not to treat.'
Maris swallowed. Her voice grew tight

'I didn't come through the Door of Death
for this. I intend my marriage to have a future
but Hardy's dying.' Sharp intake of breath
from Glasses, 'Oh no, we don't do dying here,
we don't allow it. The terms of our charter

expressly forbid it. I need the ill ones treated.
In business terms, they are my cash cow.
I think of each patient as a nursery bed,
flesh is the richest soil I know,
and sickness is simply the crop I grow.'

Wilson cut in, 'And what kind of growth
kills off its valued host too soon?'
He glared at the mother, who stifled her mirth.
Wilson continued, 'I should have read the signs,
I know who she is, this concubine...'

But Maris grabbed the Administrator
by the lapels. 'Are you out of your mind?
This woman says you're having an affair.
Are you?' 'No, I always go for blondes...'
But now the mother had laid her hand

proprietorially on his back
and nuzzled into him, seductive, sure.
Glasses was taken totally aback.
'You don't know it yet but I'm already under
your skin.' Appalled, he stared

at her in disbelief. 'No, it can't be true.
That wasn't the bargain. We all pay
for protection from you and your retinue.
I bribe you well to stay away
from me and immediate family.'

The woman chuckled. 'I can't be bought
that easily.' Then she dropped her bombshell.
'My love, I want the security codes
for Patient Records. Or I'll have your girl,
just as I promised.' Glasses went pale,

'What's going on? I don't understand,'
said baffled Ichabod. 'Do tell!
Am I missing something?' Then came a sound
that filled them with terror. Something foul
was pulling itself in heavy coils

towards them. 'Baby!' cried the woman in rapture.
'I'll save him!' said Ichabod and flew
out to passage. Wilson: 'I should have known her...'
Maris turned to her and said, 'What *are* you?'
The woman answered, 'You already know.'

Think how in Mozart when a sextet
starts a big aria and, all stood in a row,
the soloists take deep breaths and let
rip, explaining from differing points of view,
how each one sees the ballyhoo.

Wilson, the theme: 'This is the Mother of Cancer.'
Glasses to Woman: 'Take the codes and go.'
Next Maris, soprano: 'You mean my husband is with her?
She has seduced him, like Calypso?
How could he?' Then stalwart Ludlow,

the bass who underpins the song:
'I've found it, the dragon of disease!'
And Ichabod, who gets it all wrong,
as usual, but in a flash he sees
his love is false and falls to his knees.

Now all together – Maris: 'I am betrayed,
all my searching has been futile
I love him, but he'd rather stay
with her on some enchanted isle.'
Bod, baritone: 'I've been a fool.'

Coloratura: 'I have the records, I can go
anywhere.' Glasses: 'Happy now? Then leave!'
Etcetera. So much for *bel canto*.
Glasses was saying, 'Or she'll eat us alive'
and Maris was crying for Hardy, her love

and Ludlow followed the trail of phlegm
and slime the oozing dragon left
behind it, as the loathsome worm
evaded them. It took no woodcraft
to track the creature to the lift shaft.

Where now? 'The lifts are out of order,'
said Glasses, 'lucky I have a skeleton key.'
So the sweating Administrator
opened the doors and they could see
the dank shaft sink to infinity.

'There's something moving above us, I'm sure,'
said Ichabod peering into the shadows,
'I can see eyes.' But the others ignored
him, trying to keep their toes
away from the edge, which gave them vertigo.

'Right,' said Maris, 'the only way is down.'
'No way, I'm off to see my doctor,'
said Glasses, 'you're on your own.'
'But aren't you concerned about the monster?
And cancer? Don't you want to find her?'

'That bitch?' A rustle. 'That's most ungallant,'
said a voice behind. The cancer mother smiled.
'No! Don't hurt me. That's not what I meant...'
She shoved him hard down the concrete well.
Glasses grabbed Maris. Together they fell.

BOOK 7

'What is the sign of the way, O Dervish?'
... 'For you the sign is that,
for every forward step you make
you will see your distress grow greater.'

FARIDUDDIN ATTAR

'Welcome to Château Despair.'
Maris was roused by a rasping voice,
dry as drought. She was bound by gossamer,
held in a web. Before her face
eight insect eyes had fixed their gaze

thinking, unblinking. A massive spider
was hanging, alert and upside-down.
This is my phobia. Once, in a fever,
I felt that a tarantula had spun
its web on my features and laid her young

in my mind. My inner ear
could hear them growing. She sat squat
on my soul and the horror of her
has never left me, nor the freight
of her terrible belly. I have fought

a long time to ignore her hand
over my visage. What is it with spiders? Horror
at unpredictable insect brains?
Disgust at hidden adult hair
grown in dark places? Or is it their hunger

for vermin? Maris heard a faint buzz
from just below her. A bumble bee
was caught and fighting but a horrible ooze
came from its organs, turned to jelly
by poison. There's the mystery

of eight legs, of which I've heard said
they're your great-grandparents and the tyranny
of family. But who counts in the dread
of ambush? It's death in ordinary
corners, no need for recherché

theories. The dying bee went silent.
Eight eyes blinked. 'Penelope
watch you.' She did an efficient
turn through a hundred and eighty degrees,
rotating the facets of diamond eyes.

'I'm Maris.' 'I follow you on CCTV.
Administrator,' she hissed, 'not your friend,
nor mine, I sspit on him. And then I ssee
you falling, so I catch you, suspend
you over shaft then sslowly wind

you up to my office.' Another hiss.
'And him?' 'I let the enemy fall.
He waste of preciouss hosspital space.
You funny on bungee. Heavy to haul,
much flabbiness, far too tall

to be beauty, like me, sso nice and sslim.
Perhaps the Mariss have let herself go.
Penelope diet while she wait for him,
her hubby. Love leave her a shadow
of former sself, no fleshy hippo,

like human.' And the spider lunged
at her wrists, undid them, so Maris had to grasp
her hairy abdomen in case she plunged
into the darkness. Ankles free, she gasped
as the spider scampered past a shrivelled wasp

and into a high-tech gallery
full of computers. 'I more than wife,
she queen of computers, Penelope.
Waiting and watching now Penny's life
since husband Odysseus took himsself off

for dirty adventures.' The spider rustled
as her forelegs pressed computer keys.
'No excuse not to wear high heels
and stockings alwayss. When hubby
come back, he expect it. So I stay

all dressed up and ready for love
in traditional tarantula style.'
Maris swallowed. 'You don't believe
in waxing, then?' 'Hairs iss how I feel
what's happening. I very tactile.'

'I'm giving beauty advice
to a spider,' thought Maris. 'Cellulite
sso nineties. Penny look nice
by sstarving, though plenty of meat
in hospital, it fall at her feet.

She desiccated but her girlish waisst
sstill trim.' The spider heaved a great sigh.
'Penelope have been loyal, chaste
sso long her voice and eyes are dry
from crying. Better than thunder-thighs

Mariss. Since hubby leave I more cerebral,
I learn to spy. I knowing wayss
of living nearly virtual...'
At that, they heard a muffled cry
from the wall, into which three bodies

were woven in a dense cocoon.
Maris tore at the tallest. Ichabod's face
appeared, wrinkled like a prune.
He grimaced and winked. 'What is this place?'
he asked. The spider hissed, 'It interface

of hosspital knowings.' Penelope turned,
adjusting the angles of cameras
so, in the flicker of TV screens
they saw patients queueing for scanners,
the concourse. 'We likes to know where enemies are.'

And so each eye kept up a separate stare,
searching the hospital's daily scenes.
Maris asked 'What are you looking for?'
'*Hiss*. Something happening out of routine.
Somebody ssmuggling a body in

or out, unofficial. Penny afraid
he leave her for good, so she miss
nothing that happen here. She laid
plans for her husband, a sspecial kiss...'
Maris shuddered. 'Why are you talking like this?'

'Penny been vigiling so long alone,
her mouth gone like insect. No need
for speaking if you've suddenly grown
eight legs. Or if your blood
turn white one day, so Penny feed

on very little.' Maris let it go
about plans for the husband and worked instead
on Ichabod's hands. Next was Ludlow
and, lower down, Wilson's noble head,
like a mummy Anubis. He shook off the threads

of the web from his coat and placed his paws
on her chest. 'I thought you were dead.
Good thing she's not a carnivore.'
'She is, but not hungry. She had me tagged and halted
my fall. But Wilson, we're going backwards.'

Lightly, the dog fell down on all fours,
sniffed at the spider and promptly sneezed.
Small hairs were flying as her legs shed fur
(very attractive). But Maris squeezed
in beside her. 'Penny tranquillise

Mariss and friends, because she need
more watchers.' The spider zoomed in
on a woodpecker nurse refusing to feed
a patient; the readings on a dialysis machine,
doctors going about their routine.

Ichabod boomed. 'Any chance of tea?
I'm parched!' The spider turned round
in a rage. 'This one greedy
and flabby. The creature appetite-bound,
not like nice skinny greyhound,

he gross.' Maris stepped in. 'He's helping me
to find my husband. But he's easily bored.'
'My God!' said Ludlow who, now he was free,
was tapping away at a second keyboard,
'this is Paris. And it knows my password.'

'Sstupid system, alwayss going wrong,
making bad choices.' 'I have to agree,'
said Ludlow, 'but this computer's strong,
holds patients' records, perhaps it will let me
look at Hardy's notes and biopsies

and say where he is.' 'Penelope's nerves
run deep through this building's sskeleton.
She grow them down wires and through sservers.
She knows things medics have forgotten,
where specimens "lost" and secrets hidden,

but Penny sso tired, can't keep awake
always, eight eyes so ssore
she need a nest of watchers to take
more shifts.' 'She wants us to become like her!'
said Ichabod. 'She'll turn us into human spiders.'

She reared above him. 'If he get fresh
with Penny, she wrap him again,
then palp him with poison. Messy flesh
not needed. All it give uss is pain.
Much better to be a moving brain

than to feel everything. Penny don't give a damn
about Odysseus, after the ordeal
of Circe. I never let that sneaky man
break me or make me go downhill,
I no wife who wait in dishabille,

I never forgive that bitch Calypso
nor Homer who tell of their affair,
so everyone know how he love that cow.
She turn Penny into voyeur.
All that embodiment, it make her fear

what it is to be trapped in meat.
Penny dread she drown in matter –
burn, she did, in hormonal heat,
appalled by softness and by moisture.
Penny decide she not be smothered,

she choose dryness, far more subtle.
With spider body we feel safe
ethereal and in full control.'
Maris paused. 'I'm also a wife,
my husband's been with that same nymph,

but I'm sure that Hardy would never choose
to stay there, that he was deceived,
enchanted. I'm not prepared to lose
him because I foolishly believed
a deceptive illness. Can't you forgive

Odysseus? I can't pretend
I'm pleased, but I want to know
his side of the story, to understand
what happened. We may soon be widows,
so why don't you and I just go

together, to find them?' At this, Penelope cringed
and hissed as though she were sputtering fat
on a fire. 'The woman's unhinged,'
thought Maris. 'Penny never   *hiss*   ever do that.'
She seemed to be having some kind of fit,

eyes rolling wildly in eight sockets.
She writhed like a hand trapped inside a glove
too tight. Suddenly her spider skin split,
frantically the creature convulsed
and then there were two, she crawled out alive

from her exoskeleton which she shed
like a piece of irrelevant debris,
which it was. You may think her mad,
this figure-hating Penelope
but, in a way, she's a lot like me.

I often leave my body's boat
to play in the bow wave. I use rhymes
to catch stray dreams that happen to float
past me. Sound's the many arms
with which I grasp the world. My good luck charm's

a spider, now I've lost my fear
of falling, as my thread of ink
has always caught me, at least, so far.
Of course, I've talked a lot to my shrink
about my compulsions but now I think

it's healthier for me to weave
a poem than to be paranoid.
It's the only way I know how to live.
So don't be too hard on the arachnid,
she and I are secret kindred.

The new, larger spider appeared stunned
for a moment. 'Quick! Look at this!'
said Ludlow. 'From what I can understand
she has a programme for parthenogenesis
in apiculture, as well as erythropoiesis!'

'Ludlow, for goodness' sake, translate
that into English!' 'That's haematology
for blood formation. And how to cultivate
bees. Why blood, I wonder? Does she eat honey?
For the life of me, I just can't see

how they're linked. But I couldn't access
a file called "Stem Cells" – the spider twitched–
'no matter which combination of keys I press.
According to the latest research,
it's the answer to cancer.' Penelope stretched

her long new legs, reached over
and, arching her horrible spinnerets,
quickly pinned Ludlow to the floor.
Showing her fangs, the spider sat
on him. 'Penny know nothing about all that...'

But Maris was furious. 'Why didn't you share
this information?' The spider looked shifty,
if such a thing's possible. 'Cure
for cancer?' Penny lisped evasively,
began to groom herself. 'Nobody

assk her,' and there was a self-pity
in her voice which made Ichabod see red.
He thrust his face into hers aggressively.
'Not many people know this,' he said,
'in a lifetime, each person has swallowed

seven spiders. I hear you're chewy
like prawns.' Penny attacked
him viciously but Ichabod threw
her against the console, but she jumped back,
was on him again. Her poison fangs clacked

around him but Ichabod had grown
much more substantial, even burly,
fleshy and solid like a Rubens man
in those paintings we skip in galleries.
Next time you're there, look more carefully.

I used to think those nudes were crass,
big female bottoms being coerced
by violent men. But now I see mass
in the body, as in the cosmos,
is simply energy, moving through substance,

that Rubens, far from being vulgar
(forget those heaving heroic bosoms)
was a great religious painter
of incarnation. As if in slow motion
Penny and Ichabod rolled round the room

and because he was fighting for somebody else,
Ichabod's form had acquired heft.
He struggled, not out of heat, but with ice
in his mind. He managed to lift
the spider off him but she turned and bit

his left hand viciously at the wrist.
'He dead! He dead!' the spider squirmed,
but Ichabod didn't let go. 'He been kissed
by Penelope, now soon he dream!'
Far from weakening, Ichabod seemed

even stronger and he held her throat
till the spider begged for mercy.
'Penny show them the only way out,
after all – *hiss* – she iss a lady,
she always help, even the chubby.

She lend them ladders and specialist ropes.
Penelope know the Hardy is down
the lift shaft and the only hope
of finding him is if Mariss can win,'
(now she looked cunning) 'a computer game

against the cancer, like patients visualise
to help them get better. We do deal:
husband's health is a special prize
for Mariss, no? A game of skill
in exchange for a life.' 'But you've killed

my Ichabod.' 'Penny throw in anti-venom
if Mariss triumph. Bargain good for her.
Her hubby back and a serum
for Thing. What matter? Mariss no dare
play space invaders fair and square?'

She cackled. Maris looked over at Ichabod.
He was trembling, his face was pale
but he was firm: 'Maris, I'm already dead,
I know it. You should take the deal.
Just do it. Please don't make a meal

of it. Fastest way is to win the game
and get the antidote.' So Maris sat
at the keyboard and chose the log-in name
'Athena.' She pressed the button to start.
First round. She saw a familiar format:

a blood slide magnified to a field
of white and red corpuscles – erythrocytes
and leukocytes, each one a world
like a planet. Ah, four lymphocytes,
nothing abnormal requiring a fight.

So she waited, breathless, for the time-lapse.
She spotted one malignant cell,
grainy, like a volcanic island's map.
She zapped it with a neutrophil.
Ludlow punched the air – ''Atta girl!'

She blinked but the lymphoma'd cloned
itself, in sinister polka dots.
It multiplied like pulsing frogspawn.
Maris used her cursor and shot
five daughter cells out on the trot

but still they came, like a Jackson Pollock
canvas, in multiples that overwhelmed
the healthy cells. Maris locked
her eyes on mauve and cleared the screen
of cancer. 'Game over.' She had won. 'Remission.'

Next up, a smear of Hardy's bone marrow.
It looked like a coastline on its glass slide,
an aerial reconnaissance photo
of channels scoured by hostile tides,
military bunkers where enemies might hide.

She chose a fort, resolved to fight
using military weapons.
She dressed her troops in a scarlet coats.
'Stop shooting!' said Ludlow, 'they're counting your guns.
Hardy's body will be over-run.

We are out-numbered.' 'My God!'
said Maris. A hundred thousand Zulus
attacking. 'Try another method.
Use your imagination, it's a tool
that always gets us out of trouble.'

So Maris left her gun to one side
and into battle sent a flock of starlings
to scour the enemy, like a herbicide.
It worked for a moment, as did her blessings,
which wheeled in the sea like a shoal of herring,

only to meet the cancer's killer whale.
She froze the water, began to repair
the damage with a shower of hail,
picking up T-cells like fallen skaters.
But cancer melted the ice with fire

which Maris blew out. Penelope spat
in disgust but the company cheered.
'Right,' said Ichabod, 'that's that.
Maris has won.' 'Oh no, my dears,
it only beginning,' the spider sneered.

They turned. An ancient city on a plain
lay before them. Penelope said, 'Let's play
Ilium. This is where – *hiss* – the real game
commences.' 'Oh no, this is the battle for Troy,'
said Wilson. His voice was full of dismay.

'But that's a poem. A city under siege.
Hector. Achilles. Paris and Helen.'
'Look, the Achaeans are massed behind that ridge
for a final attack.' 'A reconstruction?'
'No, I fear, our eternal condition.'

'Don't worry! This time I will defend
the city,' said Maris grimly. 'I feel
sure I can change the story's end.
All it takes is some force of will.
I'll hold off the Greeks, at least until

reinforcements arrive.' 'You have no time.
Remember, cancer's already insside
the city. Odysseus leap fully armed
from the horse,' hissed Penny, overjoyed.
'Your body iss Troy and you're always destroyed.'

'Wait a second,' said Ludlow, 'keep a cool
head. There's something in the back of my mind.
I studied Greek and Latin at school,
and that, strictly speaking, isn't the end
of the story. There's hope. I think you'll find...'

Penelope exulted, took up the thought.
'Top markss to Ludlow. Troy finally fell
to a Greek who had to be brought
back from an issland where he'd been unwell.
Very kind of you, Maris, to heal

93

Philoctetes, archer. It was hiss arrow
that ruined Troy.' They saw his figure
approach the citadel and, flexing his bow,
release a shot of great mythical power.
Helpless, all they could do was stare

at catastrophe and, even worse, to realise
that it was they who'd brought it there.
Penelope crowed. 'Now Thingy dies!
With prisoners, Penny now be ssure
to get her revenge on immature

Odysseus. Ilium's halls lie open, in flames!'
Penelope sang with horrid delight,
'The way walls breached is never the same
but always a thrill at this ancient site
to watch the men I humiliate.'

Suddenly a familiar voice
cut across her. 'Maris, this is Philoctetes.
Don't listen to her, it's a double cross.
Hardy is far from dead. He's on his knees
but you can still save him. Follow the bees!'

Have you ever heard a spider scream?
It's worse than a nail on a new slate floor.
'I knew it!' said Ichabod. He grabbed four limbs
and munched them. 'Now my spider score
is eight!' Penny squirmed and swore.

The archer continued, 'She's full of hate.
Take some of her ropes and abseil down.
She isn't Penelope, she's one of the fates.
You need to go deeper underground.
Move quickly, Maris. It's nearly too late.'

BOOK 8

The dimension of soul is depth (not breadth or height) and the dimension of soul travel is downwards.

HERACLITUS

The body is a big sagacity. An instrument of thy body is also thy little sagacity, my brother, which thou callest 'spirit' – a little instrument and plaything of thy big sagacity.

NIETZSCHE

The bottom of the shaft was wet, walls stained
with streaks of mould. They could find no door.
Ichabod was in obvious pain
and rested on the concrete floor.
His skin was clammy; an orange ichor

flowed in his veins and he felt cold
to the touch. 'Hold on there, son,'
said Ludlow kindly. 'That was very bold
to bite a spider. We'll get you medicine.'
At that, a wartime klaxon

sounded and two men wearing gas masks
like those they used in World War One
stepped forward. 'Whose is the task?'
they asked in muffled unison.
Sleeves rolled up, in rubber aprons,

they looked like Red Cross surgeons.
Their nails and hands were stained deep red,
but not with paint. 'My friend needs attention,'
said Maris, approaching them. They ignored
her completely. 'This is as I'd feared,'

said Wilson but, before he could explain,
they asked, 'Who is to give blood sacrifice?'
and waited, impassive. 'What do they mean?'
asked Maris, frightened. 'There is a price
for going further into this place.'

'Which is?' 'The Underworld.' 'But I thought
that we were heading for the car park.
Hell can't be real,' said Maris, with effort.
'It is. And there isn't another way back
to the living.' 'Is this some mortuary lark?'

'This woman requires a rite of passage
to visit the shades,' said the medics. 'In her stead
someone must bear their collective rage
at the living. Upon whose head
shall this ritual be enacted?'

'They sound more like priests than doctors,'
commented Ludlow. 'You should let me go
with them.' 'But we need a medical hunter.
Philoctetes said we should follow
the bees,' said Wilson. 'I'm ancient, ergo,

it should be me.' 'But you're her breath,'
insisted a weary Ichabod.
'That would be sending her to her death,
which is not the point. If they want blood,
they can have mine. Besides, I'm fed

up with changing. I've had so many lovers
I'm ready now for the really big one
who fancies you always and doesn't care
if you haven't shaved or your zip's undone.
I'm finally ready to settle down...'

'Stop it!' said Maris. 'Please be serious
once in your life. I would never ask you
for this. I want you to stay here with us,
we'll find a way round this stupid taboo.'
'Maris, I'm finished. No, don't argue,

listen to Ichabod. Don't feel sorry,
I never do anything by halves.
I've tried too much in this old body.
Together we've had a bit of a laugh.
Now let me buy you time, my love,

to find your Hardy. Sometimes you smile
when you think of him, your voice goes soft
and tender and I can't help but feel
a little jealous. Sure, I'm tough,
promiscuous, but I've had enough

sensation. I can conduct amusing affairs
but after a certain point I'm always away.
Do you know how extremely rare
is a proper marriage? Of which you can say,
'I have loved and am loved so deeply

my real life's not here with me
but with my partner'? I can be fickle:
one fault copied in your DNA
and suddenly I'm your worst enemy.
Face it, Maris, I'm unreliable.'

'No,' she cried. But Ichabod stood,
and faced the priests, 'Lead the way, I'll follow.'
He patted Wilson, said 'Be good.'
The greyhound honoured him with a bow.
He nodded silently to Ludlow.

The surgeons led him into a room
behind what looked like bullet-proof glass.
They heard every word through an intercom.
'What first?' asked Ichabod pleasantly. 'The eyes.'
'Ah yes, a pair of fresh corneas

for someone.' They set on him. When he turns back
he's blind, with deep bloody hollows
from which two streams of tears run black.
'What next?' Slow motion. Maris throws
herself at the glass, but now our hero

can't hear her. 'Let's proceed
to major organs.' The surgeons cut
a crescent moon in Ichabod's side,
from which blood wells, a scarlet comet.
They hack at him and throw their loot,

a kidney, casually into a metal dish.
Maris's soul, she learns, is tied
to Ichabod's body. With each new gash
she twists and feels the agonies
of the body opened so its insides

steam in the cold. Now they want his liver.
They see the trap of his rib cage open
and Ichabod sinks to the floodlit floor,
the priests pursue their vivisection
and Maris is Mary at the crucifixion,

Ludlow supports her, because the sorrow
is simply too much for a person to bear.
'And, last of all, it's the bone marrow.'
Now they suck at him, like the nightmare
in Fuseli's painting. And somewhere near

a passage opens and there's a way through.
Ludlow drags Maris to the Underworld,
she's howling with grief because she knows
that, compared to the body, the soul is cold,
the best part of her self's been killed.

*

Darkness, blankness and gut-wrenching horror.
They move through the murk. She hears Wilson breathe
lightly beside her, reacting to danger
he senses ahead of them. Now shadows seethe
formless, but part to let them enter a cave

lit eerily by a sickly light
they can't place. Wilson's hackles rise.
Ludlow presses a hunting knife
into Maris's hand. Their eyes
flex and struggle. What *is* that? Fungi?

Or some kind of mineral, like quartz
shot through the rock? Suddenly, they're felled
from behind by massive force,
a monster flexing its armoured tail.
They're surrounded by reptile, foul,

unravelling. In the gloom the dragon slithers,
glowing like larva, a stinking rhizome
oozing a milk whose bitter odour
makes them gag. They slip on its slime,
are dazed as it flexes gargantuan limbs

trying to slay them. Wilson bites down on scales
but is shaken off like a harmless flea.
He continues his baiting, he barks and growls
with cries of savage ferocity.
Ludlow watches then, methodically,

works out the dragon's anatomy,
gathers Maris to him. Talons slash
around them but he dodges a way
up the torso of suppurating flesh.
They climb the thorax on a clotted mesh

of pus. He lifts her to the dragon's throat,
which screeches, like a thousand jet engines,
with animal terror. 'This is the target.
Be sure to thrust the dagger in
deep where the hide is velvet-thin

and show no mercy.' Maris hesitates.
'Do it, Maris! or he'll shake us off!'
Even though Maris is desperate
she just can't do it. 'Use the knife!'
Instead, she rests her head on the rough

hide, and feels a familiar pulse
beneath her ear. She closes her eyes
a moment and, on sudden impulse,
kisses the life that underlies
the beast's exterior. Petrified,

she waits to feel the coup de grâce.
It never comes. The cave goes still.
'Ah,' says Ludlow, 'mater familias.
I should have known you were out of my class.'
The cancer mother, now a femme fatale

enters, ball gown slit to her elegant hip,
a clinging bodice of crêpe-de-chine,
scarlet gloss on bee-stung lips.
She moves with arrogance and feline
ease, caresses the dragon, who entwines

the tip of his tail in her waist-length hair.
'I see you've met my beautiful son,'
she croons. 'Isn't he a wonder?'
'What is he, then, aside from dragon?'
'My offspring, fathered by infection.

Isn't he gorgeous?' And she strokes
him fondly. 'He has more life
in him than all of us. You should have struck
him, Maris, with your little knife.
You'd have killed your husband. Perhaps a relief,

if you were truthful.' The dragon simpers,
slithers towards the soothing voice.
Unfolding in front of her he whimpers
like any infant, he wants to be close
to his mother, to kiss and touch her face.

'I could still kill him,' challenges Maris.
'Doesn't my baby have just as much right
to life as your husband? Is it a vice
to want him to marry and to replicate?
It's just as valid for us to mutate

as for you to grow. We're versatile,
adapting to life is our party trick.'
'You *kill* us!' 'That's incidental detail.
Humans! Always moaning about getting sick,
so typically anthropocentric,

no understanding of super-success.
Have you ever watched the cell division
of cancer? From looking, you'd never guess
it wasn't an embryo, a vision
of babies to come. We're not aliens.

Cancer, the enemy, is you.
No wonder you hate us, you're afraid
of each other, of your own shadow.'
Maris toyed with the dagger's blade.
'That all sounds fair. But could I persuade

you to leave my husband? If we gave you room,
would you and your offspring, in return,
slow down perhaps, give us more time
together?' 'Negotiations always break down,
I find. Look, since before you were born,

102

I've been breeding champions from a tumour lab
in the nineteen fifties and my line's
prolific. You won't find flab
on my children because they're lean,
fit-for-purpose cell machines,

still energetic, showing no signs
of softness. We're the Olympic elite
of life forms, and we always win.
I'm sick of hearing you humans bleat
about losing. Life's a competitive sport,

why shouldn't I, as an athlete, exult
in my triumphs? After all I tower
over other mothers. I can make an adult
cry like a child, a sober man slur
or dance in torment, if I prefer...'

'You bitch!' retorted Maris. 'Oh, am I really?
Just because I don't tolerate fools,
is that my fault? Does any one ever thank me
for the way I wake up people
to the lies they've been living? How I let fall

the scales from their eyes before they die?
For the deathbed reconciliations?
How I remind you of the simple joys
like clouds and daffodils? Do I get delegations
of citizens expressing their appreciation

for spiritual services to mankind?
Like hell I do. People think it all comes easy,
but I work very hard. I wouldn't mind
if I were some slattern or if I were lazy...'
The mother whipped herself into frenzy.

'Being exceptional can be very lonely.'
'Perhaps what you need is a little rest,'
suggested Maris. 'No! At the top of the tree,
no slacking's allowed. I *have* to be best
or it's a disaster. It's shit or bust.'

'Sounds to me as though you're bone weary.
Who are you trying to impress?'
The mother paused. Her voice became teary,
'I have been under a lot of stress
Recently, and I have to confess

I'm tired of struggling. There's no end in sight.
The one thing I can't do is die,
ironic, isn't it?' 'What kind of parasite
destroys its host? Explain to me why
you can't refrain from killing the body

that supports your life?' 'I'm like the scorpion
crossing a river on the back of a horse.
She stings her friend and they both drown.
That's how I am. I've got no choice.
I'm driven by the most basic force,

by life itself. Maris, come down. There's nowhere
to go.' But Maris hesitates
and sees in the dragon's amber stare
an invitation, something intimate.
She leans and her body penetrates

his hide. Inside she's privy to his pain:
her skin, her teeth, her joints. She can hear –
not people – but everything in between
them happening. Love and fear
build a palace that only appears

to us in glimpses, feels like a ruin
but, seen as a whole, its architecture
glitters, a glorious palace, not to live in
but visited rarely. The dragon spoke to her:
'Take no notice of my mother.

She tries her best. Find the stem cell garden,
there you'll discover what's fundamental,
the real drive behind creation.
I am the centre of this hospital
and yes, in the end, I may be fatal

but, Maris, this is my secret treasure:
my heart is an ancient grave. Two lovers embrace
in death, skeletons turned towards each other,
each skull smiles at the other's face.
This love is the white-hot furnace

in which you'll find Hardy. Be on your way
quickly before I change my mind
and do as my mother wants and kill you.'
The hurting stopped and Maris found
herself in the cave again. She looked around:

the dragon's skin was coated in jewels
and, instead of a stinking worm,
the monster was glamorous, beautiful.
Maris jumped down. 'Thank you, ma'am.
We're off.' With a look of frank alarm

the mother stepped in front of the three,
said calmly, 'Oh no, I don't think so.
I wouldn't suggest you try to defy me.
When I'm aggressive I can swallow
the strongest man in days.' 'Hello!'

said an impossible voice from behind.
'I'm beginning to think you're a bit of a flirt.'
It was Ichabod, fatally wounded and blind.
'Maris did warn me. I'm very hurt,
it seems you've treated me like dirt.

Come here! Let's dance a final tango.'
He grabbed the mother. They fell to their knees.
'Maris, take the others and go!'
Cancer attacked with vicious energy,
he fell to a swarm of killer bees.

BOOK 9

Coming is real. Going is real.
What you do in between is a game.

ANNAMAYYA

The present moment is a powerful goddess.

GOETHE

Have you ever wished that you could stop time
and examine the world while it's perfectly still,
picking its pockets? The metre's ticking and I'm
stuck on the Underworld. I could steal
from translations of Dante and spend a while

doing the devil and Virgil, 'Abandon all Hope',
but you've read that already in other books.
I even devised a more modern trope.
The entrance is check-in, Charon's the bloke
who drives the dead, who are travelling folk,

to the airport, where the baggage carousel
is out of order. You get the idea:
flights are cancelled, all the hotels
are booked. Demons are terrorists wielding fire,
the damned have no papers and diarrhoea.

Very contemporary, very timely,
the runway's closed, due to fire or ice.
But this won't do because it's fancy.
R.S. Thomas – I can hear his voice –
told me once that I should choose

between fancy and imagination.
I know it's the latter that I revere,
so the hell-as-an-airport idea is gone,
but I may well use it later.
Now I'm taking the risk of not being clever.

This is the Otherworld. It isn't hell.
I'm no Orpheus, plucking the usual lyre,
it's a Celtic *Annwfn* and I'm a cell.
The note I'm seeking is the DNA
of talk. My body's the paper

on which life writes. Like music and film,
poetry excels at close-up and slow-motion,
it alters how we see space and time,
makes us their masters by changing their signs
for a while. This is why art is medicine

of kinds, although I'd take the chemo
as well as iambic tetrameter,
if I were ill enough and had to.
One thing's sure, a poet's no doctor,
but part of what a good life's for

is reaching outside of your own body.
This can mean partners and children, but some
take up residence in the city
of words and make a hospitable home
from wider linguistic chromosomes.

There's no such thing as a single bee
in nature or, if there is, it quickly dies.
The greatest achievement of humanity
is language and this is the body to which I've
made my commitment, to the hive

of speaking. In this poem's cosmology,
my Otherworld is a place to one side,
not higher nor lower. Reader, will you grant me
your breath? Because I may have died
by the time you read this, and I need a ride

in your mind. It's only for a little while.
Think of yourself as scuba gear,
state-of-the-art, of course, because style
means stamina. No, there's little danger,
if I can work out where to go from here.

*

They found themselves on a barren strand,
a great wind buffeting the shore,
so violent they could barely stand.
It was as if a demented creature
was beside itself, found everywhere

unbearable. They spotted a pier
and moved towards it gingerly.
'I don't see any Underworld here,
do you?' asked Maris. Out in the bay
the wind was raising wisps of spray

like ghosts who turned in tormented eddies
then died back to water, sinking like sand
in a dusty desert. It appeared the sea
was burning. 'I don't understand
this weather,' said Maris, leaving solid land

to walk the jetty, feeling brave,
inching over the lively water.
Beneath her the jostling, chaotic waves
made her giddy. 'This atmospheric pressure's
weird,' said Ludlow. Savage cats' paws

teased the currents. 'I suppose being ill
is this unstable.' Uncanny fog
sank towards them down a barren hill.
With it came the smell of crags,
sundew rotting in clammy bogs.

It settled like the creamy head
on a pint of Guinness. The air grew dank,
touched them so deftly that they edged
out on the pier, and instinctively shrank
from the all-annihilating blank.

But out in the offing, the buffeting wind
raged ever harder and a water spout
took shape and began to wind
its way towards them, its transitional throat
moaning with force. It finally smote

their platform and, with a roar
caught them up inside its maelstrom,
whirling them, pell-mell into thin air
then, ears popping, it spiralled them down
into the waves. There is a skin

of mind-altering, exquisite suffering
between life and death, just like the surface
of the sea, the shock when entering
the airless prairies of the abyss.
The companions fell together, weightless

as corpses. Their blood was singing,
lungs bursting but soon they found
they could breathe, just as the dying
are deep-sea creatures being drowned
in the thin atmosphere of land.

Like stranded dolphins, we keep them moist
with dampened towels and blankets until
the weight of oxygen on a labouring chest
is impossible and they find they have gills
for another medium. Or like a seal

wife whose drenching night-time sweats
show where home is. Morning reveals
her outline in salt on marital sheets.
She leaves at last for the joy of neutral
buoyancy, the supported fall

into the Otherworld beneath the waves.
Maris watched the grains of sand
like gold in the water. She gave
Wilson a look. 'Don't leave me behind,'
she thought. He answered, 'I understand,

I hear you speaking.' 'That's odd,' she thought.
'Not really, you and I are one,
it's easy for us to communicate,
I'm part of your internal conversation.'
'What about Ludlow?' 'Medical man.'

They grabbed him. He gave *Thumbs up* and all three
sank from the tumult into new ease,
their bodies adjusting to weaker gravity
and instinctively, they moved with grace
into deep water and timelessness.

They landed softly near a shipwreck.
Maris listened to her own breathing.
They waited and, slowly, through the murk
they saw a shoal of shadows approaching,
not the dead but those half living,

even on land they carry a weight –
fathoms of water. 'These are depressives,'
said Wilson, 'they live without light.'
'But how can these people be only half
dead?' 'How can you *not* be, if you're fully alive?'

retorted Wilson. Maris stretched out her hand
to a man unable to smile or speak,
but her natural gesture was overwhelmed
by internal refractions. She missed his cheek
and watched a human being sink,

then he was swept by colder currents
to somewhere darker. The friends explored
the shipwreck. There, figures leaned
exhausted on a rocks, bits of broken propeller.
'These people have forms of dementia,

a crime against time. Nobody minds
a toddler's amnesia, we find it funny,
the endless repeating of nursery rhymes
can be charming. Not so that infancy
in geriatrics. Keeping company

is all we can do as parents regress
into forgetting who their children are,
what food is for, or how to dress.
This is death with the living. And over there,'
Wilson gestured, 'are treatments for cancer.'

Maris made her way to a sunken van
with fish in its windscreen, bright as cartoons.
Patients were waiting. Each one had been stung
by the asp of a blood test. In hospital gowns,
they looked like initiates. 'Is Hardy among

this monastic order?' Maris searched
but couldn't find him with a bald head
from chemo. Yet others were scorched
by radiotherapy, where they willingly died
in parts of themselves, so they could survive

for partners, children. A white-haired woman
darted towards them. 'That's Marie Curie,'
said Wilson. 'Discovered radium.'
A swimmer in life, she was at ease
underwater. She requested news

of her work. 'I hear that the gamma knife
is much more effective, a precision tool
compared to radium that took my life
but earned me fame and my Nobel.
Does that which killed me, make others well?

No, my dear, don't get too close.
I'm radioactive. Polonium burns
me still, not even the ocean can cool
the heat of nuclear decomposition
that powers everything.' She turned

and glided away, on a thermocline
of interest only to the dead.
'She's always been my heroine,'
said Maris. The companions drifted
deeper and noticed that the seabed

was sloping downwards towards the gloom
of steely waters. Natural light
turned metallic and a plankton bloom
made seeing difficult. Ludlow cried out
when the gloaming parted and they caught sight

of a soldier emerging from a cloud of gas,
wearing a mask like the head of an ant.
He stopped, looked round and revealed his face.
'Who are you?' asked Maris. 'I'm Sergeant
Ludlow,' he sighed. 'Is this the Salient?

Oh no, I'm forgetting. It's quite elsewhere.
This isn't Ypres, I recall, and I am dead.
It takes us all some time to recover
from dying, though why I should return to this field
I don't know. I was injured here, not killed,

joined by war to the larger body
of men who've mixed their flesh with mud
in battlefields everywhere. I'll never be free
of that wound, it will forever link my blood
to richer harvests round Mametz Wood.'

'You were very daring to join the gas corps,'
Maris, surprised, heard Ludlow say.
'Not really, I didn't know enough to fear
the wind in those pre-mustard gas days.'
'They use it now in cancer therapy,'

said Dr Ludlow, 'an internal Somme
at cellular level, and so it's saved
hundreds of thousands who've overcome
malignancy and have achieved
the truce of remission.' 'Grandson, you still live.

I've learned the body's greater than the soul,
if briefer. It's not true that desire
ends with dying. What would I not give to feel
my skin raised to goose-bumps by evening air?
Or to smell the roots of your mother's hair

as I used to daily? Now I have no tale,
no narrative, no transformation,
nor work to do. I'm restless, volatile,
a member of that rootless nation,
the dead, whose endless mass migrations

wear me to nothing.' The soldier wept,
exhausted by the eternal sorrow
of the disembodied. And then he slept
and slowly he and his pack were swallowed
into the ooze that means no tomorrow.

They wandered into a gloomy reef.
Wilson went ahead but turned, aghast
at what he saw. With inconsolable grief
he howled. From the depths the massed
canine dead began to file past.

They all moved slowly and emerged
made large by water – legions of dogs who fought
in wars not their own. Some were messengers
in trenches, many were shot
with their owners. Then those who submitted

to vivisection. Bosun, Lord Byron's
dog. Those who pulled the sleds
in the Antarctic. Then the silent thousands
of greyhounds disposed of when they grew too old
to race, butchered with a bolt to the head.

Laika, the mongrel who died in orbit,
Belka, Strelka and Little Bee,
stifled, then burnt to small meteorites,
Mushka, Damka – Little Lady –
all run with Sirius now. The dogs that died

saving their owners from water or ice.
A terrier torn apart by pit-bulls,
defending his children. Dogs that had no choice
but starve, the ones who were faithful
beyond all reason, waiting outside a hospital

for dying owners. Wilson cried.
You think a dog's unable to shed tears?
You're wrong, I've seen it, in the eyes
of a spaniel whose leg was caught in wire
until we freed her. Saddened and sobered,

they swam down further into water's grain
to a deep-sea smoker, where volcanic heat
stripped out everything but a strain
of basic bacteria. In abyssal night
misshapen fish spoke out in light:

eat or be eaten, fluorescent displays,
life-forms as delicate as lace
but harder than diamond here sky weighs
like death. Wilson eased his pace,
said solemnly, 'Now we're at the place

where things that never lived are seen.
Some say they're myths and chimeras.
The human mind, as you know, is a screen
onto which we project many wonders
and, if we're lucky we might see *her*.'

'Who?' 'Helen of Troy.' 'She didn't exist,'
said Ludlow. 'Wasn't she an eidolon?
Doctor Faustus lost his soul for a kiss
from Helen, a daemonic vision.
She was an idea. No flesh-and-blood woman

could've caused such madness.' 'She was virtual,
an image of such attractive youth
her presence demolished all other ideals.
Beauty's no more than transcendent health,
symmetric features, a sign of wealth

in the genome. Helen, nevertheless, *is* real.
The camera sees her in James Dean, Monroe –
fleeting glimpses – no individual
can bear her for long. Violence follows
her footsteps.' 'Tell her to show

herself,' said Maris. 'I want to see
the form of perfection that Paris chose,
the eyes that made it worth razing Troy.
I want to see the glory we all lose,
though we never possess it.' They scanned the shadows.

Nothing. An underwater breeze
made them shiver. Then a dynamic shimmer
silvered the water. An electric charge
thrilled through Ludlow, made Maris quiver.
It was a feeling like spring fever,

the excitement of making fierce love.
It was like the scent of new-mown grass,
it was delirium. Maris felt herself alive
like a comb of cells with surplus
sweetness, dripping with rapturous

honey. And suddenly the black
was burnished, filled with a pulse
which, to the ear of her ear, came back
like the faintest music of sensuous dances,
such as the wild extravagance

that moves kelp forests with the hiss
of everything tearing but then made whole
by its own movement, which is bliss.
Maris felt newly viable
vigorous, fresh and pliable

as corn in a field, which you can hear grow
on summer nights, if you care to listen.
Maris sat down, overcome with joy
and, in the mud, saw something glisten.
She reached out her hand. A ring with a stone,

black diamond set with flaming opals.
It slipped on her finger like a promise,
a blessing, a ritual, a formal betrothal
to new life made in dust and detritus.
As Helen of Troy, the goddess passed

in brightness so keen that it was cruel,
you'd give your life for a brief affair
with such smarting. Merely feeling well
was nothing compared to being this aware.
You could die for her and she wouldn't care

or save you. Maris heard: 'Love isn't enough
to rescue anyone. You need the principles
beneath everything.' Then the goddess left.
The three ascended, tracking the bubbles
of breath and found an anchor cable

leading above them to the bobbing cloud
of an awaiting neat black curragh.
Wilson stationed himself at the prow
and the boat made weigh, though nobody steered
or thought to talk to one another.

They sailed a long time. The travellers stared
for hours at the water and saw the places
they knew in their youth and were hypnotised
by thousands of dear and indifferent faces,
crushed by the waves' incoming staircases.

Maris looked down at herself. The world went through
her body, as if she were made of smoke or mist.
They could see horizon through her tissues.
Her body was porous, nor could she resist
the tiniest fluctuations of light,

and now she found that even pain
passed through her, with the weather.
Life showered her like shimmering rain.
It was dusk and Maris could no longer remember
the colour of Hardy's eyes, his features,

but that didn't stop her pressing on,
even though she'd lost his gravelly voice,
it didn't matter. She hummed a song
about sailing without chart or compass.
Soon they saw the Island of the Blessed.

BOOK 10

Human life begins on the far side of despair.

J.-P. SARTRE

There is a land of the living and a land of the
dead, and the bridge is love, the only survival,
the only meaning.

THORNTON WILDER

An island appears every seven years
out of the mist. Its name is Hy-
Brazil. No one knows where it wanders.
It is a place of coming-to-be,
of life outside the living body.

Maris, Ludlow and Wilson all stood
as the black boat's flat-bottomed hull
scraped on sand. Their mood
lightened, they raced each other up the hill
to the shade of an eucalyptus grove, quite still

in the midday heat. A cicada's note
held up the foliage. Suddenly a man,
immaculate in a pin-striped suit
and a great coat, sporting a boyish grin,
said, 'Welcome, friends! I'm Aneurin Bevan.

I have been chosen to be your guide
for this stage of your journey.' 'Your portrait's hung
by the stairs in the hospital, just outside
the clinics,' said Maris. 'You, a young
minister when the NHS had just begun.

You're on top of a mountain.' 'That's Ebbw Vale,
my constituency! I'd walk the moors,
reciting poetry, it helped to heal
my stutter.' Ludlow, clearly in awe
gushed: 'Mr Bevan, you're a giant figure

in my life. Founder of the National Health
Service – medical, dental and nursing care
for everyone, regardless of wealth,
free at the point of use. It meant the poor
for the first time could call a doctor

without any worry.' 'It wasn't free,
but paid through taxation. I was very proud
of the wigs and the wheelchairs, artificial eyes,
the millions of glasses and hearing aids
dispensed by the service. Has it survived?'

'It has, and it's thriving. Expenditure
is close to a hundred and fifteen billion.'
'In all?' 'No, only last year,
but there are problems.' The Welshman's
eyes grew moist and he had to turn

away with emotion. 'It was very tough
persuading the doctors that the state
didn't want to abuse them or the trust
between them and their patients. The debate
was fiery. But fifth of July, nineteen forty-eight...'

'I hate to cut across this cosy chat,'
said Maris impatiently. 'But I haven't come
through spiders and hellholes in order to wait
while you two stand talking. Ilium
is burning, remember. I have to get to him,

my Hardy, with some kind of stem cell
before next week. This is bizarre –
a dead politician dressed like a swell,
going on about government.' 'My dear,'
said Bevan softly, 'I died of cancer

brought on, I suspect, by the terrible strain
of fighting for the very best
healthcare for everyone.' 'There you go again.
Can't politicians ever give it a rest?'
Ludlow was stung, grabbed hold of her wrist

and, furious, hissed, 'Maris, do you know
how much needless suffering this man
prevented? How much sorrow
he saved, how much bone-grating pain
he healed? Show some respect. Without him

where would Hardy be now?' 'No, she's right,'
said Bevan. 'I like to reminisce
about my achievements, I can lose sight
of the task in hand. Love is ruthless
and so it should be. But, to business.

This is the task with which I'm charged:
Maris, you have everything to lose.
At the heart of this island is an orchard,
a stem cell garden. You are to choose
which cells the haematologist will use

to transplant into Hardy, so he can grow
his own defences and become well
behind high hedges of new bone marrow.
This is the hazard: cancer stem cells
grow in the garden too and will kill

him faster than usual, being malignant
and potent.' 'I don't understand.
What *is* this place?' Bevan was silent
a second. 'This isn't solid ground
but a place of potential, actions that resound

forward through time and, sometimes, echo
back to affect events. This island floats
through space and time. Here we foreknow
the future's genome. It's like a boat
riding the waves of an implicate

ocean behind the things we see.
Things can happen and unhappen at once,
then happen again. Probability
waves break on our beaches, the first surge destroys,
the second restores. Nobody knows

how such flux happens. Uncertainty
is this island's principle. Each cove
both exists and doesn't. The geography
is everything possible, because love
believes in it all.' The trees of the grove

sighed as if an enormous sea
were in them, a surge of suffering
from which we take life and buoyancy,
whose spray is an eternal spring
of breaking, dying and becoming.

It spotted with rain. 'We should depart,'
said Bevan. 'What if Hardy's already dead?'
asked Maris grimly. Nobody answered. Her heart
sank to her boots. They looked ahead
and the quantum island had expanded,

it seemed to them. Mountains rose
in the distance. They watched a bee
buzzing round Maris. Bevan asked, 'Do you know
about the hives?' 'Not really, Philoctetes
told us to follow bees.' The worker was heavy,

rested on Maris's foot, where it settled,
its trousers bulging with pollen stuffed
like money in clothing. Its velvet
thorax was glossy. When it had rested enough,
it flexed its stained-glass wings and took off,

with Maris chasing. 'Wilson, let's go!'
and the greyhound followed, the two men behind
still talking with passion and gusto
about medicine and how we're still behind
continental Europe. They descended

into a wooded valley where giant umbels
of hogweed frothed. 'How's your mythology?'
asked Bevan. Around them nightingales
vied with each other. 'Antiquity
is a hobby of mine. At university,

of course, I did read Hippocrates.'
'Would you care to meet him? It could be arranged,
you only have to petition the breeze
in these groves of Hellas.' The shadows changed
and, as the path they were following plunged

into a gorge, ahead they saw a figure
waiting to join them. 'Do you mind if I talk
to my predecessor?' asked Ludlow. He was so eager
Maris couldn't say no. 'Talk as you walk,'
she answered briskly. 'Keep us awake

as we travel.' 'I've always loved conversation,'
continued Bevan. 'Now you're being modest.
You were a famous rhetorician
and orator.' 'I have been a fortunate guest
here, among the best from ages past

you wouldn't believe the company!'
The Greek stood up and bowed to greet
the travellers. 'This is a dream come true for me,'
fawned Ludlow, who nearly fell at the feet
of the father of medicine. 'This summer heat

is bad for headaches and encourages sloth.'
His tone was soothing. 'Tell me, young doctor,
is it true that students still take my oath
when they qualify?' 'They do, although it's more
like a list of duties, a general charter

than a vow to be religious and chaste.'
'That's a shame,' sighed Hippocrates. 'My friend,
how else can a doctor give a boost
to the patients he's sworn to attend?'
'Did you know your name became a brand

for what everyone thought they knew
about classical healing?' 'I can't take credit
for most of my writings. The men who followed
me wrote them, though there is much merit
in 'Life is short, Science is long' – that's it!'

'I liked the chapter "Airs, Waters, Places",
observations on outer and inner weather
and how they're related. And "Prognosis"
is still important.' 'Medical care
is all about stories. What's happening here?

What's likely to happen? In the end it goes badly
for everyone. Are mortality rates
still a hundred percent for everybody?
Even for doctors? If so, let's celebrate
while we're still alive!' 'You should rewrite

the Aphorisms,' said Ludlow. 'The first one's fine,
but what about cupping a woman's nipples
to stop her periods? I draw the line
at that.' 'I didn't say it!' Hippocrates giggled.
'And another thing,' Maris quibbled,

'doctors should never tell those lies.
"A little discomfort" means "It really hurts".
"It's nothing sinister" is "Prepare to die".
and "You're depressed" means "I know very well
you're awkward, please take these pills

and go away". Why is the patient's time
always disposable? "I'll be right with you"
means "You read this crap magazine while I'm
doing something". Those clinics' queues
kill me.' Ludlow then asked, 'Is it really true

that, as part of doing the patient no harm,
it was recorded that you once said
a doctor's task was to entertain
the patient till he or she was fully recovered?'
'That's something I firmly believed.

It's not doctors who heal, we merely help the body
to perform the work, which it does on its own.
That process is a mystery.'
Maris joined in, 'Don't death rates decline
when doctors strike and surgeons down

tools?' 'That's right,' Ludlow nervously laughed.
'It's natural to want to intervene
when someone is suffering.' 'It's sometimes enough
to be with your patient and to place their pain
in a story.' The valley's luscious green

gave way to a drier, broader plain
of open prairie across which swifts
swooped like Mother Carey's chickens
over an ocean. 'I have a gift
for you, Ludlow. Sometimes all that's left

for a physician is to make a new tune
from the hours of waiting, to recompose
the story in a broader tone,
so doctor and patient can both lose
themselves, be found by the muse

of time rearranged.' He drew a boxwood flute
from his cloak. 'If you're about perish,
remember that music will help you fight,
when things seem hopeless. I've found that flesh
will do more for love than you could wish,

that music rouses when all else fails.
Take it and use it. Others will follow
if you find the melodies that heal
yourself. Play soft and low
and, Dr Ludlow, you will know

my breath joins you, and that of every other
physician.' Ludlow took the flute and bowed.
'I am not permitted to travel further,'
he said and waved goodbye as he watched them go.
'Great men sometimes have little ego,'

commented Ludlow. They trekked, it seemed, for days
over a plain that led to a sandy desert.
All night they saw the feverish eyes
of wolves. Wilson lay, a sphinx, alert.
Around the fire Maris overheard

Ludlow telling Bevan about cancer.
'We're using radiotherapy and chemo
to produce remission in childhood leukaemia,
chemical warfare on rogue bone marrow,
but there's something still that we don't know:

why cancers recur when we've already killed
the tumour with, say Cyclophosphamide.
We think there may be cancer stem cells
surviving the cellular genocide.
We need to find out where the strong seeds hide.

Stem cells in general offer great hope
for all kinds of radical therapies –
Parkinson's disease and, I don't think it's hype,
it can help with spinal cord injuries,
severe burns, childhood diabetes.

You could grow your own organs. Come and see
the stem cell harvest.' 'That is a promised land
for others,' said Bevan, 'not for me.'
Maris slept little but later she dreamed
that night embodied itself and formed

a gleaming blackbird and it sang to her,
a wedding ring around each dark eye:
'Give me a message for Hardy, my dear,
I'll fly to him, wherever he lies.'
'Tell him his darling is near by,'

she answered, 'then give him a kiss,
spread your dark wings over his hair.
Let your golden beak take on his disease,
then fly to the sun and burn it there
in a chrysanthemum of fire.'

She slept and it was already late
when they left, began the long descent
towards a castle. The path was desolate,
all around them moorland burned.
Stunted, smoking hedges leant

into the weather. Under them, granite
glinted and its gravel crunched
like glass underfoot. They reached the outer limit
of a city walls and Bevan sat down, hunched,
on a wall while they took a final lunch

of water and berries. 'This is where I leave
you, darlings. It has been
the greatest pleasure. Remember: love
is strong as stem cells, has its genes,
inheritance as rich and unforeseen

as fallen fruit. Its potency
helps to determine the very form
of how we can live. Maris, choose wisely.
Remember: you need to grasp the nettle of time.'
He turned, and started his long, lonely climb.

BOOK 11

Haile be thou, holie hearbe, growing in the ground;
all in the Mount Calvarie first wert thou found.
Thou art good for manie a sore, and healest manie a wound,
in the name of sweet Jesus, I take thee from the ground.

1584 BLESSING FOR GATHERING OF SIMPLES

Lady, this is a *pārijāta* flower.
Human beings can't get it.
Śaci, Pārvati and Sarasvati wear it every day.
You need to know this, since he gave it to you,
and since you are life itself, outside his body.
No one can equal you among all his sixteen thousand wives.

NANDI TIMMANA

'Wilson, I'm frightened.' A daunting wall
surrounded the garden, it seemed, on all sides,
barbed wire on its apex, impossible to scale.
'Ask for a door to take you inside,'
the dog suggested. So, in her mind's eye

Maris imagined a simple arch.
The three of them entered, only to find
not lush and well-tended gardens but a parched
vista – disordered, abandoned ground.
You could see that it had once been grand:

the eye was drawn by formal flower beds
laid out in complex boxed parterres.
Gazebos and pergolas had led
the attention to a central water feature.
All this was more than half obscured

by scrub and brambles. Japanese knotweed
smothered the outlines, sending astray
all design as it went to seed.
'Don't tell me we've had to come all this way
for this,' said Maris, in dismay.

Ludlow said, 'This is Hardy's body,
his lymphatic system.' 'It's a total mess.'
Maris touched a choked-up gully.
It was full of rotting, tarry foulness
that stank with rankness as it deliquesced

to black ooze running thick and sticky.
'No wonder he's ill, if he has this crud
in his system. I think it's up to me
to clear this jungle and restore his blood.'
And Maris tackled the ground where she stood,

tearing up handfuls of vegetation,
taking her vengeance out on ground elder
and couch grass that grew in such profusion
it robbed all else of earth and air.
The weeds grew back like Hardy's tumour.

She started again, picking up litter –
crisp packets, condoms, bits of plastic dolls,
half-rotted newsprint. 'I must work harder,'
she told herself but thick twitch cables
cut her hands. The earth was marbled

with roots, like fat through meat.
The couch revived – the very soil
was riddled with the parasite.
It rose as fast as Maris pulled
it out.' She thought, 'These stubborn tendrils

are stronger than I am.' One single tear
fell to earth, its tiny weight
bending a leaf of maidenhair
which added liquid, to create
the start of a mercury rivulet.

When love's so weary it hopes for nothing
it's at its strongest, though it feels no power.
It pushes, persists and starts its streaming.
Clay relaxes to the touch of moisture,
it gathers force, pushes sand grains over

and, on its way, is fed by everything
it touches, now it's flowing over,
it surges and begins to sing
words of mercy in the throats of gutters,
thoughts translated into sudden flowers.

In silence, Wilson watched it all:
how Maris's sorrow had cascaded
in tiny channels and careful rills
laid out to delight the hot and jaded,
and how they babbled into deepening pools

cooling the noon, how rhythmic fountains
pulsed into life. He saw with wonder
how water's silver glistening vein
filled the garden with a refreshing timbre,
gurgling, laughing out an Alhambra

of myrtled terraces and colonnades,
pavilions and star-tiled belvederes,
ponds with carp that hug the shade,
groves with persimmon trees and private arbours
quick with the flash of white kingfishers

and, finally, Maris lifted her head
and gasped, astonished, as around her she saw
chamomile lawns with fragrant edges
of lavender, plantain and plumbago.
She rose to her feet in order to follow

a gill which chattered, gushed and bubbled
past statues, follies, then changed its tune
to the minor key through a yew tunnel
then disappeared deep into underground cisterns.
They came to an orchard. It was late afternoon,

the shadows long. In a panic, Maris ran
to the centre, casting desperately about.
'Quick! Help me to gather what cells I can
for Hardy before our time runs out.
How do I know which is wholesome fruit

and which is cancer?' 'This one has mites,'
said Ludlow. Another tree had scales,
a Pippin the corky flesh of bitter pit.
There were aphids, wingless moths and weevils,
and apple sawfly. 'It's impossible to tell,'

cried Maris, anguished, 'which stock is healthy,
which is diseased. I need a greyhound's nose
to sniff out potential. Wilson, can't you help me?'
'I can smell cancer, but here I'm confused.
Maybe it's these, or it could be those...'

Maris turned and walked to a grave
at the orchard's fringe and sat against the headstone
only to find that it was a hive
and far from dead. She could hear a drone
which seemed to grow stronger, a golden tone

of ordered work and honeyed halls.
She closes her eyes. The keynote splits
into a chord whose timbre swells,
throbs round her head a golden helmet.
The mind of the hive decides to admit

Maris inside it, into the dark
 of ambered labour, and in its gleam
Maris hears the collectors of nectar speak:
'A hive is an endless conversation
of life with itself. Our sequestered queen

tastes the topaz of where we went.
Your marrow, human, is a honeycomb,
so sweet.' Maris feels herself fragment
but isn't alarmed when she looks down,
to see bright bees crawl through her bones.

Now she perceives her friend who was felled.
'Ichabod! Is it really you?'
'Maris, my dear, you've reached the Field
of Cells, where messages can echo
forwards and backwards. Bodies don't always flow,

like chronology, in one direction.
Stem cells undo the mistakes of time.
They can create a fresh new season
for Hardy. Choose with love, what looks infirm
may be the elixir when the chimes

are ringing.' She was surrounded by the smell
of summer pastures, which began to hum
in scents of meadowsweet, thyme and tormentil,
a hot and sensuous diapason.
'Ichabod, will I see you again?'

He laughed with a mirth that was warm and full.
'Who knows? Don't worry, I am safe
in pointillisms of potential.
You'll see me often, because my life
is out of my body. Now be a good wife

and find your husband a new immune
system which he and you can grow
together. Beauty's only a clue,
a hint. The secret's in the come and go
between us. Time ceases to flow

then starts again. Now Maris, hurry!'
The hive released her and she looked around,
focussed this time on the nearest tree
leafless, fruitless, moribund.
The church bells then began to sound,

blossom opened and the fat buds tore –
controlled explosions, like shouts and screams
with pollen spittle, words for 'Me!' and 'More!'
The dead tree now wore bridal cream,
flower flesh with petal wounds

and suddenly the sacred falls in snow
like light on branches and – fast-forward –
fruit ripens under white's cold shadow
gorgeous, vermilion-flushed as blood.
Reality is open wide,

ice slides off branches. The impossible
starts happening in shake and shimmer.
Time slows, time's poised and time stands still,
the snow reveals the tracks of a hare,
the hare itself and nothing there.

A single stem cell, ripe as a moon
pulses above her, thrumming, whole
and pluripotent, as if she alone
needed healing and she watches it fall
into her hand like a miracle.

And in a moment will begin the thaw
but not yet. One last peal,
this orchard still is Tir na n-Óg,
the kingdom of youth, where filigree
of snowflakes glint in the espaliers

and now it melts, saplings drip
and there are oranges and nectarines,
pomegranates, red as rosehips
and figs in their sweet and succulent prime
And Maris says, 'Now let's go home,

I'm ready,' she said, hugging her windfall.
But, like a gathering storm
the bees come after her. She called
the others. Ludlow waved his arms
at the insect fog which quickly formed

in clouds around him. 'Head for water!'
he instructed. Even hirsute Wilson
was being stung. But as they ran they saw,
beyond the orchard, stem cells being sown
in special beds – infinite cordons,

tissue nurseries for the rarest breeds
of motor-neurones, basal ganglia,
cold frames protecting delicate seeds –
experimental medulla oblongata.
fibres of irises in every colour,

a heraldic terrace stocked with chimeras,
tentative creatures that don't live long,
poor things. Relieved, they reached the castle cloisters
where, to the sounds of ancient plain-song
they saw where teeth were being grown

in petri dishes, the papery rustle
of skin sheets hanging, developing
like photographs. Cardiac muscles
beating already, and designer strings
of enzymes, talking and glittering.

One thing she saw made Maris turn pale.
A doorway was ajar to a guarded room:
a model was strung up on a scaffold
of infinite genes, a human simulacrum
enhanced, so perfect that illness was dumb

in its pathways. Before she could tell
the others, the future's door swung shut
excluding them. They ran before a swirl
of bees like smoke, their stinging as hot
as wrath, precise and urgent.

They went for the cellars, found the crypt
flooded with water, its low-arched ceiling
studded with stalactites, which dripped.
Panting, the three stood still, all listening
to the sound of trickling water.

The surface stilled. One graceful vault
joined its two halves to make one eye
which stared right through them. Wilson felt
a growing unease. 'Can you tell me why
the water's showing a starry sky

when we're inside?' the dog enquired.
'This is odd, I can't see my face
in the reflection.' Nobody replied.
Of Maris and Ludlow there was no trace.
They had been torn into outer space.

BOOK 12

The word 'sea' is small and easily uttered.
They utter it lightly who know least about it.
A vast ancient terror is locked in the name
Like energy in an atom.

GEORGE MACKAY BROWN

These are the only genuine ideas: the ideas of
the shipwrecked. All the rest is rhetoric,
posturing, farce.

ORTEGA Y GASSET

Open doors of time! open hospital doors!

WALT WHITMAN

They were floating in orbit above the earth.
Something glinted, caught Maris's eye –
a space-station jewel turning far beneath
them, fragile, unbearably tiny
under the curve of earth's round belly.

So Ludlow and Maris, hand in hand
made haste for the module. It seemed they could move
in the vacuum at will, command
some resistance. They were both alive,
though neither was breathing. The capsule dissolved

into earth darkness. Now they could hear
the panic of several system alarms,
all wailing, summoning engineers
to different crises. 'Try to stay calm,'
warned Ludlow but Maris was frantic. 'It's him,

I know it. The transplant's gone wrong.
Hardy, I'm coming!' Fumbling, she found a porthole,
peered in. 'The chemo they use is very strong,
to kill off the cancer.' The station started to roll,
its gyros disabled. A jet of lime-green glycol

leaked from a vent. There was a fire on board
and batteries were critically low.
Fans closed down. Then they emerged
into the sunlight and Maris saw
a figure – Hardy – opening the door

of an airlock, in a bee-keeper's suit.
He inched out, feeling for solar arrays
to turn them so that sunlight
might revive the station. Maris made her way
towards him, urgent. But, suddenly

she saw that Hardy had lost his hold
on the station and was floating loose,
a dead man in the brilliant cold
of space. She screamed but, of course, her voice
didn't carry. 'Don't get too close,'

warned Ludlow, 'you'll do more harm
than good. He's had it. Hypoxia.
It's a good way to go.' She grabbed his arm,
pulled him towards her. 'First, euphoria,
then oblivion.' She raised his gold visor,

cried out in shock. It was full of bees
in a boiling waggle dance. They roiled
all over him. 'Cellular activity,'
said Ludlow. 'There's no one inside
the suit,' said Maris, utterly horrified.

Maybe not then, but this is what Hardy saw
from his dying: Maris, bending over him
and, behind her the vibrant, dazzling core
of the sun, rich and red as haemachrome
at fifteen million degrees. He was overcome

by the knowledge that everything 'out there'
was, in truth, his own body. We're filaments
of light, we're talking with everywhere
at once, and we were never meant
to be thought of as single, lines to be bent

in the space-time continuum.
That's prose. No, it's more like the drive
of poetry. It's as when I rhyme,
there's always a nano-second before I've
chosen a word when I perceive

all its homophones at once
before the end-word's probability wave
collapses, before I take a chance
on one meaning, when my mind revolves
with the quantum mechanics that makes stars evolve

from the tiniest jitters. We're born
to catastrophe. Galaxies fly
away from each other in identical forms.
Matter never sees fit to die
and if life is the transfer of energy

from one state to another – this poem from me
to you – then this continual exchange
must be our purpose. Infinity's
birdsong continues just beyond the range
of our human hearing. Love is the hinge

on which it all turns, the continuous verve
of protons decaying into tau muons,
it's the lurch in the stomach as we feel the curve
in space made by gravity. It goes on and on,
it's physicists guessing about a Higgs ocean,

that sea in which, maybe, we all swim.
The theory goes that it gives us mass
(also to squealing swifts as they skim
like neutrinos over the adoring face
of an evening river, which matches their grace),

that stuff which interacts with gravity
then on to inertia provided by weight,
the drag in the muscles which helps us feel
our true condition. Suffering creates
substance which nothing annihilates.

We're lucky, weighed down by rocks of care
at a particle level. Hardy watched the exploding sky
stare down at him blankly. I use the life of stars
to fight against tumours. Each night I try
contracting my father's to the density

of a neutron star which, in its turn
becomes a black hole and disappears
behind its own event horizon.
I'm afraid this won't work. Cancer reappears
in jets of raw plasma from a nebula

of hot, new stars, a nursery.
I love him and, therefore, he's not alone.
I keep on trying. As for immunity,
two systems are much, much better than one.
It may be that Hardy heard the tone

that will heal him. Some say that energy
vibrates, that stuff's made up of superstrings,
that physicists study harmony
and that particles aren't billiard balls, things,
but notes, all matter a coherent song

for many voices – gluon, graviton –
harmonics on a musical scale
played by the universe, a tune
so complex and so beautiful
we can barely perceive it as it swirls

through stars like semen that thicken to curds,
a foetus. Or, maybe, like a stem cell
striking a tuning fork, the chord
that leads to all others. An aureole
of light through smoke, the diastole,

galaxies calling on every wavelength
like a once mighty but now-dispersed choir
whose distance only increases the strength
of its voices, for atoms always remember
their origins as one, together

before the explosion. And what do they say?
'I am I! Clamo! Clamavi!' They proclaim
it over and over in endless joy
so articulate even the vacuum
is seething with singing, its natural idiom.

Remember how the Venerable Bede
describes our life as that of a sparrow
flying in winter? It wanders inside
a feast hall with an open window.
Heat, food and light. Then it passes through

back out into darkness. How much more
seldom in space do we find the life
that could support us. Even more rare
is a marriage, and Maris wasn't a wife
to give up. No, she was charged by grief

and, ignoring Ludlow she, oh so tenderly,
drew Hardy's corpse in its airless coffin
back to the station. Did you ever see
Sandro Botticelli's drawings
of Dante and Beatrice in Paradise, floating

weightless? He clings to her, they rise
upwards. She supports him and they glide
together higher, so that he can gaze
on heaven. Dante seems half cowed
but Beatrice smiles, for she has saved

her poet. Maris brings Hardy to the cargo bay,
makes sure he's safely inside the lock,
undresses him, uses emergency
thrusters to turn the whole station back
to its proper orbit. Soon they have contact

with Ground Control and comms are restored,
the batteries charging. She closes her eyes,
sees scatter plots as particles explode
on her retina, the rain of cosmic rays
in which we all live. Two worlds collide

and Maris perceives, beyond the photons
that light up the world, the pull of dark matter,
a tide that washes over those who mourn
for others. It makes the world cohere
but plunges it into deep, sunless water.

Now Maris is tumbling though the endless roar
of a breaking, rending, dangerous sea,
but she lets it have its way with her
because now she has the humility
to trust in her spirit's buoyancy.

Peace, Love and Death. Of these three
Peace is the least, the greatest one is Death.
When someone chooses it willingly,
Death includes the others. It's the roughest path,
but the kindest. Maris can't breathe

but notices Ludlow climbing a rope
of bubbles. Wilson floats past,
limp and lifeless. Maris loses all hope
for herself, she knows she can't outlast
his expiry. In despair, she grasps

the scruff of his neck. 'I'm passing out,'
she thinks, relaxes. She can hear wails
and something she thinks is the regular beat
of propellers through water. Wilson's tail
twitches. They surface. The hospital pool.

Ludlow grabs them and pulls them out.
He pummels Wilson's heart. Nothing.
He tries massage. Maris cradles Wilson's snout
in her lap. The time he'd bought her was too long
for even a hero. She starts her keening

over his body, sways on her knees.
Suddenly, a massive jolt
shocks through the building. Wilson sneezes.
And again. 'I think this boat
is sinking,' he says. 'We should depart.'

No dog likes kisses, but the noble hound
put up with some slobbing as Maris squealed
with delight. 'Enough! This ship has run aground,'
Wilson persisted. 'That's no big deal
at low water,' said Maris. 'I fear the hull's

been pierced.' And, as if to confirm
his diagnosis, the whole ship heeled.
Maris caught sight of a gang of germs
fleeing. 'I tell you, the vessel's holed
under the water line. The keel

can't take the longitudinal strain.
Time to evacuate. Abandon ship!'
commanded Wilson. 'No! I've got to find
Hardy first.' 'This is a death-trap.'
'I'm not leaving without him,' Maris snapped.

150

Haematology. Maris recognised
Hardy, lying pale and wan
in a corner. Wearily, he opened his eyes,
saw her, complained, 'Where have you been?'
His tone was disgruntled. 'You took your time...'

Before she could answer, the whole world slid
to one side, sending drips and trays
flying. Something went 'Pouf!' and the power grid
shut down. 'We can't afford to stay,'
said Ludlow. 'Everybody, follow me!'

But nobody stirred. They were far too ill
to care about danger. Hardy turned
his face to the pastel-coloured wall.
Maris bent over him, at first concerned,
then angry. 'Hardy! Get up!' she said in a stern

voice but Hardy had his mind
on other problems. 'That goes for you all!'
she shouted at the patients behind.
She pulled him up. His limp arm fell
onto a pillow. Maris called him from his hole

to his pole, but her husband simply didn't care.
'I'm not having this, us being shipwrecked
after everything else. I've come too far
to lose him now. I never wear black.
I'll carry him out on piggy-back

if I have to. Ludlow, Wilson, can't you rouse
those others? I'm going nowhere
without them all.' Wilson tried to philosophise
the patients upright. Indifferent stares.
Ludlow deployed his best bedside manner.

Ditto. Another lurch. 'She's down at the bows,
this hospital can't stay upright
much longer.' Maris turned to Ludlow.
'Why don't you try that wooden flute
that Hippocrates gave you?' He pulled it out,

uncertain. 'Thing is, Maris, I haven't a clue
how to play it.' 'Just do it, Ludlow. I'm quite sure
he'll help you.' So Ludlow softly blew
over the mouthpiece. His embouchure
drew a long note so clear and pure

that patients sat up. They were surprised
into action. He found a beat
he liked and began to improvise
an Irish reel. Hardy's skinny feet
begin to tap. So, quickly, she sat

on the edge of his bed, took his weight
on her back and lifted. She was shocked
that such a large man should feel so light
but she followed Ludlow, who was now locked
into a melody with such attack

patients were rising, like the recently dead,
to trills and grace notes. Ludlow gathered
everyone to him. He went round every bed.
People pulled drip stands like tango partners
beside them. Patients with asthma

found they could skip, the music took the strain.
The body's percussive, just think of the noise
it makes on its own – the large intestine.
You can't make people move, but if they choose
to dance, that's different. Now Ludlow schmoozed

the nurses and doctors out of other wards
to join them. Maris saw the Cleaner
helping a mother. Above her a bird –
red underside, the neurotic woodpecker –
was drumming, leading them to drier

decks on the liner. And from the hold
came Cardiac patients, behind their consultant,
a bass drum thumping out a bold
heartbeat with the assurance of stents
replaced and working. To this confident

whumping Neurology added high-pitched bugles,
joined by the piccolos of the deranged
and demented. They came all higgledy-piggle,
displaying urgency and range,
all entered the music and came out changed

by syncopation, when the crowd was joined
by Endocrinology's jazz ensemble.
Orthopaedics brought a flügelhorn
of pain, which the orchestra was able
to modify to a bearable level,

by clever cadences which reframe
agonies, taking them by the throat,
making them sing, recruiting time
to be on our side, for once, and beating out
new modes of thought, as metrical feet

enable a poet to undertake
the longest journeys without getting tired.
Maris noticed the weight on her back
getting more heavy as Hardy stirred,
taking an interest now, directing her

past hazards and obstacles. The dead don't understand
language but they stood aside
for Orpheus when he went underground
to fetch Eurydice, his bride.
He persuaded Hades with the eloquent sound

of his singing, led to the incredible
woman behind him. But he doubted it,
turned back to check and lost it all.
This poem has given me the loping gait
of a marathon runner, allowed me to concentrate

over a distance. Hardy climbed down
and started walking, leaning on Maris's shoulder.
He looked behind. Patients in gowns
were carrying stretchers, helping each other
to escape. He stood up straighter,

fell into step with the notes' commands
confirming and strengthening his heartbeat,
retuned his immunity. He took Maris's hand
and held it. Good doctors co-ordinate
the body's rhythms, orchestrate,

a place to live. For we perform
our health, like music, in ensembles,
within the limit of our genome.
Bad health is contagious. We can only be as well
as our loved ones so, when they fall ill,

we suffer. At the head of the parade
Ludlow rode the dragon of disease
in triumph. Now well-being spread
around them. Maris met Philoctetes
and they embraced as a salty breeze

refreshed her. Spontaneous remissions
broke out, a benign epidemic. If vigour's a grace,
extended in time it becomes a heaven.
And they saw it in glimpses: a Mughal terrace,
lovers on balconies, jasmine, the bliss

of clarity, fountains, being maharaja
of your own body, the flirting eyes
enjoying brightness, the inherited splendour
of palaces, gardens, a second paradise.
Rain pavilions and peacocks' cries,

courtesan laughter from secret places,
a fever of happiness which is an outbreak
of health, invading the public spaces.
The boat received another shock,
the strakes began breaking. From the deck

they could see dry land. Phil shot an arrow
tied to a rope. It hit the sand,
as a lifeline useless, so Maestro Ludlow
strengthens his music. He tunes the band
an octave higher. Everyone blends

even closer and throws a harmonic ramp
over the fatal rocks into thin air,
so women and children are able to jump
to safety. All cross on a final cadenza,
couples and families greet each other,

the hospital sinks beneath the weight
of false expectations. The amnesiac sea
closes over it. Survivors cut
bracelets from wrists so they are free
to go on living. Here ends my story,

but not Maris's marriage. 'I was lost at sea
for ages,' said Hardy. 'My darling.' Maris smiled,
suddenly feeling absurdly shy.
'Yes, it took me a little while
to find you.' So, does Hardy stay well?

Can't tell you. But when he lifted her hand
to kiss it he began to cry
to see a new ring: opals, one black diamond.
Maris comforted him and whispered, coy:
'A present to us from Helen of Troy.'

NOTES

6: Adapted from Anon, 15th century in Gerard Benson, Judith Cherniak & Cecily Herbert, eds, *Poems on the Underground* (Constable, 2003), p.214.

BOOK 1
7: Quoted in Julia Blackburn, *Old Man Goya* (Vintage, 2003).

BOOK 2
15: William Osler, 'Nurse and Patient' in Osler's *'A Way of Life' and other Addresses with Commentary and Annotations*, ed. Shigeaki Hinohara & Hisae Niki (Duke University Press, 2001), p.190.
Thorwald Dethlefsen and Rüdiger Dahkle, *The Healing Power of Illness* (Element, 1990), p.4.

BOOK 3
31: 'Sonnet (II)', *The English Poems of George Herbert*, ed. C.A. Patrides (Dent, 1874), p.206.
Robertson Davies, *The Rebel Angels*, p.255.

BOOK 4
45: Dēvara Dāsimayya, *Speaking of Siva*, tr. A.K. Ramanujan (Penguin, 1973), p.106.

BOOK 5
57: Dethlefsen and Dahkle, *ibid*, p.55.
Richard Grossinger, *Planet Medicine* (Shambhala, 1982) p.103.

BOOK 6
Second Fruits, 1591. Quoted in Gavin Maxwell, *The Ten Pains of Death* (1959), epigraph.

BOOK 7
79: Quoted in Dethlefsen and Dahkler, *ibid*, p.93.

BOOK 8

95: Quoted in James Hillman and Thomas Moore, *The Essential James Hillman: A Blue Fire* (Routledge, 1990), p.22.
Friedrich Nietzsche quoted in Joanna Field (Marion Milner), A Life of One's Own (Virago, 1990), p.194.

BOOK 9

107: *Classical Telugu Poetry: An Anthology*, tr. & ed. Velcheru Narayana Rao and David Shulman (University of California Press, 2002), p.149.

BOOK 10

121: 'The Flies', tr. Stuart Gilbert, *No Exit and The Flies* (Knopf, 1948), p.149.
The Bridge of San Luis Rey and Other Novels 1926-1948 (Library of Congress, 2009).

BOOK 11

133: Quoted in Mircea Eliade, *The Myth of the Eternal Return* (Arkana, 1954), p.30.
Classical Telugu Poetry, p.181f.

BOOK 12

143: 'The Sea: Four Elegies', *The Collected Poems of George Mackay Brown*, ed. Archie Bevan & Brian Murray (John Murray, 2005), p 168.
Walt Whitman, 'The Wound-Dresser', *The Complete Poems*, ed. Francis Murphy (Penguin, 2004), p.335.

ACKNOWLEDGEMENTS

Many scientists have helped me with this book, for which I'm extremely grateful. Professor Sir Martin Evans, Nobel Laureate 2008, advised about stem cell technology. Professor Stephen Tomlinson and Professor the Baroness Finlay of Llandaff acted as mentors. Paul J. Smith, Professor of Cancer Biology and Rachel Errington, Senior Lecturer in Biomolecular Imaging at Cardiff University, answered my many questions about cancer cells. Professor Mike Edmunds gave me tutorials in cosmology and particle physics, and I'm extremely grateful to him for setting up a term for me as Poet in Residence at Cardiff University's School of Physics and Astronomy. I would also like to thank the staff of the University Hospital of Wales for letting me observe their work.

For the idea of the three doors, I'm indebted to Kirsti Simonsuuri's poem 'Night Opens Three Roads.'

A fellowship from the National Endowment for Arts, Science and Technology allowed me to research the poem. I'm deeply indebted to the Wellcome Trust for a Sciart Award and for a continuing dialogue about the biomedical sciences. An Arts Council of Wales Creative Wales Award gave me the time to write. Parts of the book were written at Villa Hellebosch, thanks to Het Beschrijf, and at the Heinrich Böll Cottage on Achill Island. I'm grateful to both for their hospitality.